MW00990428

DAVENANT GUIDES seek to offer short and accessible introductions to key issues of current debate in theology and ethics, drawing on a magisterial Protestant perspective and defending its contemporary relevance today.

THE TWO KINGDOMS

A Guide for the Perplexed

BY W. BRADFORD LITTLEJOHN

CONTENTS

1 INTRODUCTION: WHICH TWO   1
   KINGDOMS?

2 THE TWO KINGDOMS FROM LUTHER   12
   TO CALVIN

3 THE TWO KINGDOMS FROM CALVIN   31
   TO HOOKER

4 CONTRIBUTIONS OF TWO-   48
   KINGDOMS THOUGHT

5 TWO KINGDOMS IN THE CHURCH   55

6 TWO KINGDOMS IN THE STATE   72

7 TWO KINGDOMS IN THE MARKET   88

8 CONCLUSION   100

   BIBLIOGRAPHY   105

I:
INTRODUCTION: WHICH TWO KINGDOMS?

FOR the past few years, the narrow world of conservative North American Reformed theology has been torn by one of its regular bouts of internecine strife. This latest round, however, holds more than the usual interest, representing as it does but one form of an identity crisis afflicting every Christian communion in the late modern world. How should we understand the relationship between the public and private dimensions of faith in the aftermath of the breakdown of Christendom and the paradigms for public faith that it offered? These, however imperfect, at least provided some framework for the intersection of Christian faith and citizenship. And of course, although the modern form of this identity crisis is new, the questions behind it are timeless: how do we reconcile loyalty to God, our highest authority, but a hidden one, with loyalty to the very visible earthly authorities that He has set above and around us? How, moreover, does our calling as followers of Christ relate to our calling as sons of Adam and daughters of Eve, our spiritual and heavenly good relate to the goods of the earth we have been called to protect and serve.

The conflict I refer to, of course, surrounds the emergence of so-called "Reformed two-kingdoms" (R2K) doctrine, which, in its contemporary form, is particularly associated with theologians at Westminster Seminary in Escondido, CA (thus the occasional moniker "The Escondido Theology"), such as Michael Horton and David VanDrunen, though its most outspoken representative has perhaps been Hillsdale professor Darryl G. Hart.[1]

UNDERSTANDING THE "REFORMED TWO-KINGDOMS" DOCTRINE

Like most movements in theology, it can be best understood by first understanding what it is reacting against. The R2K theorists have their sights set on a trio of boogeymen within the conservative Reformed and evangelical world: theonomy, neo-Calvinism, and evangelicalism (although a broader array of foes, such as the emergent church and N.T. Wright, are sometimes in view as well). Of these, theonomy (also known as

---

[1] David VanDrunen's *Natural Law and the Two Kingdoms: A Study in the Development of Reformed Social Thought*, Emory University Studies in Law and Religion (Grand Rapids: Eerdmans, 2010) offered what was widely taken to be an authoritative historical survey offering support for the doctrine, while his *Living in God's Two Kingdoms: A Biblical Vision for Christianity and Culture* (Wheaton, IL: Crossway, 2010) offered a more systematic and practical sketch of how he intended the doctrine to work in the life of the church. Darryl Hart articulated a similar viewpoint in *A Secular Faith: Why Christianity Favors the Separation of Church and State* (Chicago: Ivan R. Dee, 2006), and *From Billy Graham to Sarah Palin: Evangelicals and the Betrayal of American Conservatism* (Grand Rapids: Eerdmans, 2011), as well as being the most forceful and articulate defender of R2K doctrine (or at least his own take on it) at his blog, oldlife.org. There have been many counter-attacks on the doctrine in blogs, magazines, and journals; a good book-length collection of largely neo-Calvinist responses can be found in Ryan C. McIlhenny, ed., *Kingdoms Apart: Engaging the Two Kingdoms Perspective* (Phillipsburg, NJ: P&R Pub., 2012).

Reconstructionism) is probably the most obscure to non-Reformed audiences. A movement that enjoyed considerable vogue among the arch-Reformed in the '80s and '90s but has recently faded, theonomy proposed a full-blown recovery of the civil laws of the Old Testament as a Christian blueprint for modern society. Any political theology short of this, theonomists claimed, was compromise with unbelief, privileging man's word above God's.[2]

Neo-Calvinism enjoys a much more mainstream recognition, including (in its broadest construal) such well-known political theologians as James K.A. Smith, John Witte, Jr., and Nicholas Wolterstorff, and serving as a dominant force particularly among the Dutch Reformed. Its card-carrying, doctrinaire membership, however, with whom the R2K theorists are particularly concerned, occupies a somewhat self-enclosed circle among conservative denominations and institutions. They are distinguished by their commitment to the public theology of Abraham Kuyper, mediated through twentieth-century Dutch philosopher Herman Dooyeweerd and North American followers such as Henry Stob, Al Wolters and Cornelius Van Til (though this latter offered his own distinctive twists which proved congenial to theonomists). In a nutshell, this tradition's slogan is "Take every thought captive to the lordship of Christ," a determination to "transform" the various "spheres" and institutions of society by grounding them upon the fundamental ideas of a "Christian worldview." Unlike theonomy, neo-Calvinism

---

[2] Classic texts expounding this perspective are Rousas John Rushdoony, *The Institutes of Biblical Law* (Phillipsburg, NJ: P&R Publishing, 1973), and Greg Bahnsen, *Theonomy in Christian Ethics* (Phillipsburg: P&R Publishing, 1984).

is concerned more with philosophical "ground-motives" than legalistic prescriptions, with the spirit rather than the letter, but it can be similarly triumphalist in aspirations.[3]

"Evangelicalism" is of course the most inchoate of the three foes, but the one that has been the target of the lion's share of the more popular level R2K writings, such as those by Horton and Hart.[4] American evangelicals are blamed for a low ecclesiology that devalues the institutional church, its ministries and sacraments, in favor of a naive biblicism that thinks there's a Bible verse for every problem, and for a belligerent political activism. Taken together, these lead to a confusion of the kingdom of Christ with worldly politics, as evangelicals insist on imposing particular understandings of what Scripture demands on voters and politicians. Of course, stated this way, such criticisms of evangelicalism are nothing new, and would be shared by many beyond the Escondido theologians. Theonomy, too, has few friends nowadays, and although neo-Calvinism may have a strong constituency both at more popular and more intellectual levels, most of its representatives would acknowledge the fairness of many R2K warnings against triumphalism—confusing our own cultural labors with Christ's transforming work in a way that places both an unreasonable burden of expecta-

---

[3] Key texts expounding this perspective include Cornelius Plantinga, *Engaging God's World: A Christian Vision of Faith, Learning, and Living* (Grand Rapids: Eerdmans, 2002), and Albert M. Wolters, *Creation Regained: Biblical Basics for a Reformational Worldview*, 2nd ed. (Grand Rapids: Eerdmans, 2005).

[4] See for instance Michael Horton's *Christless Christianity: The Alternative Gospel of the American Church* (Grand Rapids: Baker, 2008), and Darryl Hart's *From Billy Graham to Sarah Palin.*

tion on Christians and unfairly denigrates the goods that non-believers are capable of achieving.

The Reformed two-kingdoms movement's chief concerns, then—a desire to re-emphasize the centrality of the Church in the Christian life, a suspicion of over-reaching claims for biblical authority and applicability, a healthy cynicism about the ability to realize gospel norms in temporal and political structures, and a stress on the wide area of commonality between believers and unbelievers in our mundane lives—all seem like salutary ones, shared by most sober and theologically thoughtful commentators. But this does not mean that most commentators would share the theological framework underlying these critiques, which rests on an extensive set of neatly-correlated dualisms: spiritual kingdom vs. civil (or "temporal" or "common") kingdom, church vs. state, redemption vs. creation, eternal vs. temporal, Jesus Christ vs. Creator God, Scripture vs. natural law. The institutional church, we are told is Christ's spiritual kingdom, in which alone the work of redemption is being carried out for eternal salvation, under the headship of Jesus Christ, who rules this kingdom by Scripture alone. The rest of life, on the other hand (and preeminently the state) is an expression of God's civil kingdom, in which there is no distinction between believer and unbeliever; this sphere serves merely for the temporary preservation of the creation order, under the government of God as Creator, and normed by the prescriptions of natural law, rather than Scripture.

Thus, although the R2K movement has gotten considerable traction from critiquing of overreaching expressions of political Christianity or cultural transformationalism, it has also encountered fierce resistance from those who fear that it wishes to throw out the baby of public discipleship with the bathwater of partisanship and triumphalism. Indeed, many critics of western evangelical Christianity have complained for years about the "Gnosticism" that they fear infects evangelical faith: an other-worldly concern with saving souls to the exclusion not only of organized social and political action, but of any thoughtful engagement with the cultural and material forms of life on this earth where we are called to witness and enact the kingship of Christ. From this perspective, forcefully articulated both by intellectual heavyweights like N.T. Wright and intellectual lightweights like Brian McLaren, the R2K advocates charged onto the scene with fire extinguishers just at the moment that a healthy passion for displaying Christ *in this world* was finally being kindled among evangelicals. Among evangelicals converted to this new world-affirming Christianity, as well as Reformed folks who have drunk deeply from the wells of neo-Calvinism, R2K doctrine has looked like a summons back to the kind of privatized, other-worldly religion that, we are told variously, is the pernicious fruit of Platonism, or the Enlightenment, or postmodern pluralism.

THE MAGISTERIAL PROTESTANT DOCTRINE OF THE TWO KINGDOMS

In the little book that follows, I will argue that both the R2K advocates and their critics have largely missed something much richer, more fundamental, and more liberating and insightful for the church today: the original Protestant two-kingdoms doctrine, as articulated by such giants as Martin Luther, John Calvin, and Richard

Hooker.[5] The Protestant Reformers, I will argue in the pages that follow, offered us a compelling account for a faith that is thoroughly public without being either triumphalistic in the civil sphere or oppressive in the ecclesiastical sphere. Their work was hardly perfect, their words not always clear, and their legacy often ambiguous, and yet their core teachings were coherent and consistent enough for us to speak meaningfully of a magisterial Protestant two-kingdoms theology that can still offer us a compass for thinking about the meaning of Christian faith and discipleship today. This theology, while certainly overlapping on many points with the more recent Reformed two-kingdoms theology, differs fundamentally not just in the answers it yields to certain questions but even in the key questions it is seeking to answer.

Consider the question of the relationship of church and state that has been so prominent in many expressions of recent Reformed two-kingdoms theology. R2K theology, in the hands of at least many advocates, offers Christians the key to endorsing the religious neutrality of

---

[5] Steven Wedgeworth and Peter Escalante, more than anyone, deserve credit for putting this forgotten perspective back on the table, exposing that both neo-Calvinism and the Reformed two-kingdoms doctrine violated the older Protestant distinctions in key ways. For some of the key earlier polemics in this debate, see Steven Wedgeworth, "Two Kingdoms Critique," *Credenda/Agenda*, June 21, 2010, http://www.credenda.org/index.php/Theology/two-kingdoms-critique.html; the collection of articles linked here: https://wedgewords.wordpress.com/2011/08/20/two-kingdoms-and-political-theology/; Steven Wedgeworth and Peter Escalante, "John Calvin and the Two Kingdoms—Part 1," *The Calvinist International*, May 29, 2012, https://calvinistinternational.com/2012/05/29/calvin-2k-1/; Steven Wedgeworth and Peter Escalante, "John Calvin and the Two Kingdoms—Part 2," *The Calvinist International*, May 29, 2012 https://calvinistinternational.com/2012/05/29/calvin-2k-2/. I am deeply indebted to their work throughout this exposition.

modern liberal politics without succumbing to relativism, because they recognize that the task of the state is merely temporal and the claims of Christ speak only to the spiritual work of the Church. It would be difficult to recognize such an account in the political theology of the Protestant Reformers, full as it was of calls to civil magistrates to be new Deborahs, Josiahs, or Hezekiahs, cleansing the church of its idols and protecting and fostering only the true worship of God. To be sure, the Reformers had plenty to say about the distinction of vocation between priest and prince, but they never suggested that one was bound to give public and institutional expression to the kingship of Christ and the other was not.

No, for the Reformers, two-kingdoms doctrine was not primarily about church and state, or even necessarily political theology more broadly construed, even if it had very important implications for political theology, which we will explore in this book. The two kingdoms were not two institutions or even two domains of the world, but two ways in which the kingship of Christ made itself felt in the life of each and every believer. As such, they were tangled up with all the various forms of "twoness" that run through Christian theology on every front: God and the world, special revelation and general revelation, redemption and creation, divine grace and human response, faith and works, justification and sanctification, soul and body, invisible and visible, church and world, etc. Theology, quite clearly, cannot do well without clear distinctions between any of these pairs, even if, equally clearly, it can shipwreck by too sharply opposing any of these two terms to one another. At each point, a delicate balancing act is in order.

Of course, good theology must also be careful not to treat all these distinctions as just different versions of the same fundamental duality (a temptation that some overzealous two-kingdoms theorists have been prone to)—merely to pick one example, we obviously cannot equate the "redemption/creation" pair with the "soul/body" pair, since Scripture speaks clearly of the redemption and resurrection of our *bodies*. At the same time, it would be an untidy theology indeed that made no attempt to map these various dualities onto one another at all. For instance, for Protestants at least, divine grace, faith, and justification all fit together well on one side, in distinction from human response, works, and sanctification, on the other.

Martin Luther's theology, for all its notorious untidiness, was particularly characterized by its attempt to tie together these various dualities within a single framework, with plenty of appropriate qualifications (though it usually fell to his successors, particularly Philipp Melanchthon, John Calvin, Peter Martyr Vermigli, and Richard Hooker, to spell out those qualifications). For him, then, and for other magisterial Reformers who spoke of "two kingdoms" (or "two realms" or "two governments," to use perhaps clearer terms corresponding to Luther's *Zwei Reiche* and *Zwei Regimente*), they had in mind not primarily a pair of institutions (i.e., "church" and "state") but something much more fundamental. Human life is not a two-dimensional map onto which the two kingdoms are drawn as a dividing line between spheres of jurisdiction; it is rather a three-dimensional reality of which the whole horizontal dimension is coterminous with the temporal kingdom, with the spiritual kingdom forming the third dimension—the vertical God-ward relation which animates all the rest. At every point, the Christian must be attentive to the voice of God as he speaks in his word, and the face of God as he presents himself in his world, through what Luther calls "masks."

When one puts it this way, it becomes clear that this dividing line must run right through the church itself. The Reformers could speak of the church, in its visible gathered form, with officers and liturgical orders, as part of the "earthly kingdom"; however, as the company of the elect, mystically united to her head, she is the fullness of the spiritual kingdom. But while the "visible/invisible church" distinction is not far off here, it is not sufficient either, for it, like the language of "kingdom" is much too static for what the Reformers had in mind. The *geistliche Regimente* was the spiritual ruling and reigning of God, His gracious life-giving action through the power of the Spirit. While clearly invisible in itself, this liberating rule makes itself manifest in the powerful reading and preaching of the Word (and that chiefly, but certainly not merely, in the context of formal worship), in the sacraments, and in the loving, faith-filled acts of the saints.

Of course, these acts of love, in which the Christian makes himself "the most dutiful servant of all," are the very stuff of which the "earthly kingdom," the space east of Eden and west of the new Jerusalem, subject to human authority and prudential calculus, is made. But this simply highlights the fact that the language of "the two kingdoms" ought not serve to neatly divvy up the various elements of the Christian life into one or another sphere, but rather, often, ought to be viewed as two different ways of talking about the same elements. We are *simul justus et peccator*, at the same time free lords and dutiful servants, at the same time alive with Christ in the heavenly places and toiling in murky paths here below, and even as we enjoy the liberty of a conscience set free by grace, we live under the laws (natural and civil) that regulate our lives with one another as human creatures. To confuse these two rules is to risk libertinism or legalism, triumphalism or despair.

In other words, when we talk about "the two kingdoms," we are talking about much more than what it means to be a Christian citizen. We are talking about what it means to live as a Christian in the world, and "two-kingdoms doctrine" is simply shorthand for the magisterial Protestant answer to that question, an answer that needs to be heard anew in every generation, but especially our own. In the short guide that follows, then, I will offer first a historical sketch in three chapters of the actual evolution of two-kingdoms ideas in the sixteenth and early seventeenth century, and their implications for political theology, ecclesiology, and Christian life. Then, in the second group of two chapters, I will turn to offer a creative appropriation of the doctrine today in the three key spheres of church, state, and marketplace, suggesting how it can shed fresh light on seemingly sterile disputes over how to live out the lordship of Christ in the 21st century.[6]

---

[6] Chapters Two and Three are based on a series of essays I wrote for *Political Theology Today* in late 2012; Chapters Five, Six, and Seven are adapted from pieces I wrote for *Reformation21* in early 2015. All have been expanded substantially for this book. I am grateful to both web journals, and their editors Dave True and Mark McDowell, for the opportunity to develop these thoughts.

II:

THE TWO KINGDOMS FROM LUTHER TO CALVIN

SIMUL JUSTUS ET PECCATOR: MARTIN LUTHER'S THEORY OF THE TWO KINGDOMS

ANY DISCUSSION of the doctrine of the two kingdoms must necessarily begin, historically speaking, with Luther. As a political theorist, Martin Luther has been variously identified as a revolutionary figure who fundamentally reshaped Western political order and as an otherwordly theological reformer whose political ideas, inasmuch as he had any, were intensely conservative and frankly rather uninteresting. Thankfully, there is a way of accounting for both assessments, for both are, in fact, two sides of the same coin—that coin being his famous two-kingdoms doctrine.

It is true that Luther generally wanted to leave political order alone to do its own business as much as possible, without too much meddling from theologians or churchmen. To this extent, he was clearly no political revolutionary in our modern sense, nor did he have an interest in making a contribution to political theory as such. But it was precisely this stance that represented a dramatic shift in how most Christians had thought about politics for centuries, and that in certain ways laid the foundations for modern liberal order. No longer was political authority to be an appendage or henchmen of spiritual authority, or for that matter its exalted vicegerent. Luther simultaneously promoted and demoted all forms of civil authority: *promoted* because princes and emperors were now answerable to no one but God alone, with no earthly rivals within their dominions; *demoted* because their task was now so very mundane, in every sense of the word: to preserve outward order, and no more, until the Son of Man should return.

Now, to be sure, we must not overemphasize the originality of Luther's ideas. The theme of "twoness" permeates the Christian political theological tradition from the beginning—"two there are by whom this world is governed"—that much seemed clear from quite early on. But despite the antecedents we might find in Augustine's theology of the two cities, or Gelasius's of the two swords, Luther's two kingdoms cannot be equated with either. A closer antecedent lies in medieval distinctions between the *forum internum* and the *forum externum*, and the innovative thought of Marsilius of Padua in particular.[1] However the "two kingdoms" remain a distinctive and unique product

---

[1] For representative texts in the unfolding development of medieval "two swords" political theology, see Oliver and Joan Lockwood O'Donovan, eds., *From Irenaeus to Grotius: A Sourcebook in Christian Political Thought, 100–1625* (Grand Rapids: Eerdmans, 1999), parts 2, 3 and 4. For Marsilius of Padua's radical assault on traditional medieval political and ecclesiological assumptions, see Marsilius of Padua, *The Defender of the Peace*, ed. Annabel Brett, Cambridge Texts in the History of Political Thought (Cambridge: Cambridge University Press, 2005).

of Luther's theology, resting as they do directly on the bedrock of his doctrine of justification *sola fide*.

This connection with the doctrine of justification has not always been sufficiently recognized in the voluminous secondary literature, which has often, with the politicizing bias of modern thought, leapt too quickly to a reading of Luther's kingdoms as two institutions—church and state—whose business must be strictly distinguished. Of course, any sensitive reader of Luther has had to acknowledge that there is rather more going on in Luther's theory than just that, but many have persisted in the conviction that *something* like this is envisioned. David VanDrunen is among these in *Natural Law and the Two Kingdoms*, where he treats Luther's two-kingdoms theory as a precursor of the Reformed version he will narrate (which he understands to be quite clearly a theory of these two institutions).[2]

In his excellent recent study Martin Luther's *Doctrine of the Two Kingdoms*, William Wright assails this tendency, calling us back to what the best scholars have always recognized—that Luther's doctrine of the two kingdoms is on the contrary a comprehensive framework on which he hangs his understanding of God, man, and society, predicated on the reformer's basic distinction between man as he is *coram Deo* and *coram hominibus*.[3] It flows, in short, from the doctrine of justification, with Luther's famous concept of *simul justus et peccator*, his conviction that the realm of appearances is very different from the realm

---

[2] See particularly pp. 55–62.

[3] William F. Wright, *Martin Luther's Understanding of God's Two Kingdoms: A Response to the Challenge of Skepticism* (Grand Rapids: Baker Academic, 2010).

of spiritual realities. Christ reigns mysteriously and invisibly over the kingdom of conscience, and no human authority may dare to interpose itself as the mediator of this rule; it is by faith alone that we participate in this kingdom, so we must not be deceived into identifying it with external works or rituals.[4] Perhaps better than the terminology of the "two kingdoms" then, the *zwei Reiche*, is that of the "two governments," *zwei Regimente*.[5] The spiritual government is that by which Christ rules inwardly in the conscience by his Word and Spirit, the realm of grace; the temporal government (*weltliche Regimente*) is that by which Christ governs all external human affairs by law, in which he works not directly and immediately, but through the *larvae*, "masks," of earthly governors and institutions. Only the elect experience the former; the latter they share in common with the unregenerate.[6]

From this it should be clear that it will not do to talk of any empirical institution (including the church) as being in the spiritual kingdom, but of course, neither will it do to suggest that any sphere of life is merely secular. As stated above, for Luther, the "secular" or temporal realm designates the horizontal dimension of human existence,

---

[4] The classic study of the relation of Luther's two-kingdoms thought to his larger soteriological concerns remains F. Edward Cranz, *An Essay on the Development of Luther's Thought on Law, Justice, and Society* (Cambridge, MA: Harvard University Press, 1959).

[5] The best analysis of Luther's terminology, and how it all fits together, remains W.D.J. Cargill Thompson, "The 'Two Kingdoms' and the 'Two Regiments': Some Problems of Luther's *Zwei-Reiche-Lehre*," *The Journal of Theological Studies* 20, no. 1 (1969): 164–85, and John Witte, Jr., *Law and Protestantism: The Legal Teachings of the Lutheran Reformation* (Cambridge: Cambridge University Press, 2002), 89–115.

[6] For an accessible and relatively concise survey of Luther's two-kingdoms theology, see Witte, *Law and Protestantism*, 89–115.

which is of course at every point subjected to the authority of God in Christ, sometimes more explicitly (as in the outward ministry of the church), and sometimes more indirectly (as in most of the work of the magistrate). Thus the church itself is just as subject to the paradoxical dualities of *simul justus et peccator* as is the justified believer. In its hidden identity before God, the church is the "spiritual kingdom," invisible as such to men, but taking visible form in the dynamic preaching of the Gospel and administration of the sacraments. In its visible, institutional dimension, as a gathered congregation that must be organized, ritualized, and governed, the church is part of the realm of what Luther calls "polity," part of the sphere of human authority which it occupies in common with the more mundane concerns of the family and the civil magistrate.

Intimately connected with this doctrine is Luther's teaching on Christian liberty, which from the beginning was shot through with this same twofold dialectic—"free lord of all, subject to none/dutiful servant of all, subject to all."[7] Inwardly before God, the Christian is not subject to the mediation of any human authority, or conscience-bound by its commands. But by virtue of this very inward freedom, the Christian cheerfully accepts subjection to the needs of his neighbor (and, because of this, to human authorities) in the outward realm. Outward matters were *adiaphora*, "things indifferent to salvation," in which human law could command a believer's conduct, but not his conscience. Thus, when Luther insisted that Christian

---

[7] Luther, *The Freedom of a Christian*, trans. W.A. Lambert, rev. Harold J. Grimm, in *Luther: Three Treatises*, 2nd rev. ed. (Minneapolis: Fortress Press, 1970), 277.

liberty did not overthrow political authority, this was not because he was carefully confining it within a sphere called "church," outside of which the conscience could be bound, but because the two governments—over conscience and over conduct—were intrinsically incommensurable. "Things indifferent" also often referred to things on which Scripture offered no direct or perpetually binding command, and which hence could be left to human discretion (whether of the individual Christian or of authorities in church and state).[8]

The foregoing may suggest that while perhaps important for ecclesiology and even soteriology, Luther's two-kingdoms doctrine was without much significance for political theology. In fact, it held profound significance for the future of Western political theory, in at least two respects. First, by rejecting the idea that the teaching office of the church could hold any kind of political power, Luther's doctrine upended the medieval political order and left the civil magistrate as the sole possessor of juridical authority. Indeed, so much so that the church itself, to the extent that it must take an institutional and juridical form (as Luther soon came to recognize after his early idealism), could fall under the oversight of the Christian magistrate, whose lay status was no longer any bar to a kind of leadership within the church. Melanchthon in particular would systematize Lutheran doctrine in this direction, deeming that magistrates could wield authority and

---

[8] For a full exposition of the complexities and debates over the notion of "things indifferent" in the Lutheran Reformation and beyond, see ch. 2 of my new book, *The Peril and Promise of Christian Liberty: Richard Hooker, the Puritans, and Protestant Political Theology* (Grand Rapids: Eerdmans, 2017).

demand obedience in ecclesiastical *adiaphora*—questions of outward order, polity, and to some extent liturgy.[9]

But if on one level Luther's reform worked to concentrate power in the hands of the princes, it does not follow from this, as many popular and even scholarly narratives would have it, that it paved the way for absolutism. On the contrary, the second effect of Luther's two-kingdoms doctrine was a decidedly liberal one, since it desacralized not merely the church hierarchy, but all human authority. No longer the executive arm of the church's spiritual authority, the magistrate could make no claims on conscience, no pronouncements on eternal matters. Moreover, since there was no longer any authoritative earthly arbiter to fix the just bounds of the conscience, the Christian individual in principle could stand as judge over the commands of his magistrate, if the magistrate sought to go beyond the realm of *adiaphora* which limited his authority. Naturally, there was a certain amount of tension between the magistrate's authority to command in *adiaphora* and the individual conscience's authority to determine when the boundary of *adiaphora* had been transgressed. Thankfully, as we shall see, this proved to be a creative tension, stimulating Protestant political reflection for two centuries to come.

---

[9] The authoritative exposition of Luther and Melanchthon's understanding of the role of civil authority in the church (and its relation to their two-kingdoms doctrine) can be found in James M. Estes, *Peace, Order, and the Glory of God: Secular Authority and the Church in the Thought of Luther and Melanchthon, 1518–1559* (Leiden: Brill, 2005).

THE TWO KINGDOMS IN THE EARLY REFORMED TRADITION

But we must move the story along, for there was more to the Reformation than Luther. In Zwingli's Zurich reformation, similar reforms came about, though on a rather different terminological and conceptual basis. Neither Zwingli, nor his successor, Heinrich Bullinger, formulated their theology in terms of "two kingdoms," nor did they share Luther's strict Law/Gospel dichotomy, meaning they were more willing to look to the Old Testament for guidance. This meant that the "godly prince," called to take charge of the Reformation of the church like a new Josiah, instructed by his "prophets," the ministers, stood absolutely front-and-center in their concept of a reformed society.[10] As we have seen, though, the "godly prince," charged with reform, was not inimical to Lutheranism, nor were the basic principles of Luther's two-kingdoms doctrine lacking among the Swiss. For them too, the core doctrines of justification by faith, Christian liberty, and the all-sufficiency of Scripture served to drive a sharp wedge between Christ's spiritual government over conscience, and his rule over civil and temporal matters by human vicegerents. The compatibility of the Lutheran and Reformed strands on these points can be seen in the thought of Peter Martyr Vermigli, an Italian reformer who spent much of his reforming career in England (on which

---

[10] See Pamela Biel, *Doorkeepers at the House of Righteousness: Heinrich Bullinger and the Zurich Clergy, 1535-1575* (Bern: Peter Lang, 1991); Daniel Bolliger, "Bullinger on Church Authority: The Transformation of the Prophetic Role in Christian Ministry," in *Architect of the Reformation: An Introduction to Heinrich Bullinger, 1504-1575*, ed. Bruce Gordon and Emidio Campi (Grand Rapids: Baker Academic, 2004) 159–77.

he exerted an immense influence) and Zurich, and whose robust political theology combined the strong Hebraic themes of Zurich with Lutheran and Melanchthonian concepts of *adiaphora* and the two kingdoms.[11]

If there was a difference between Luther and Zurich on these points, though, it was that the latter was not disposed to emphasize the "freedom of a Christian man" quite so much as the former. In principle, both the Zurich and Wittenberg reformers agreed that the Ten Commandments were a restatement of the natural law, and the other laws of Scripture binding only as particular applications of this natural law (and thus potentially revisable in different circumstances). In practice, though, the Zurich reformers were much more likely to continue to look to Biblical law to govern the Christian life, and never indulged, as Luther sometimes appeared to, in flirtations with antinomianism, but highlighted from beginning the need for the Reformation to include thoroughgoing moral reform.[12]

This potential legalism, however, was tempered by two key factors. First, Zwingli and Bullinger maintained a clear commitment to the notion of *adiaphora* and did not adopt the biblicist principle that would require direct biblical warrant for any church ceremonies—much less

[11] See W.J. Torrance Kirby, "Peter Martyr Vermigli and Pope Boniface VIII: The Difference Between Civil and Ecclesiastical Power," in *Peter Martyr Vermigli and the European Reformations*, ed. Frank A. James III (Leiden: Brill, 2004), 291–304; and W.J. Torrance Kirby, "Political Theology: The Godly Prince," in *A Companion to Peter Martyr Vermigli*, ed. W.J. Torrance Kirby, Frank A. James III, and Emidio Campi (Leiden: Brill, 2009), 401–22.

[12] See Paul D.L. Avis, "Moses and the Magistrate: A Study in the Rise of Protestant Legalism," *Ecclesiastical History* 149 (1975): 148–72.

civil laws. The temporal kingdom was one ruled by discretion and prudence, even if Scripture offered many principles and precedents to be followed. Second, their emphasis on the role of the godly magistrate in overseeing a reformed society actually included a safeguard against the kind of perfectionism that would try to make the temporal kingdom match the perfection of the spiritual. There was only so much a magistrate could do to morally improve a sinful society without provoking division and resentment, and hence order and decency, rather than purity, must be the mark aimed at. More radical reformers, such as Conrad Grebel and Balthasar Hubmaier, saw such forbearance as half-heartedness, and the Anabaptist movement was founded on a determination to pursue rigorous discipline within the visible Christian community, erasing as much as possible the gap between the church invisible and visible, the spiritual kingdom of Christ and its temporal manifestation.[13] Indeed, it is at this point that we can see how misleading it is to depict the two kingdoms, as many do, as essentially a matter of church vs. state. On such a reading, by rejecting altogether the notion of the Christian magistrate and insisting on a separate and self-governing church, the Anabaptists would seem to be *more* two-kingdoms than anyone. But this is not at all how the magisterial reformers saw it, seeing rather in their emerging pacifistic ethic a conflation of the internal and external

---

[13] See Kenneth R. Davis, "No Discipline, No Church: An Anabaptist Contribution to the Reformed Tradition," *The Sixteenth Century Journal* 13, no. 4 (1982): 43–58.

planes of Christian ethics, a confusion of the two kingdoms.[14]

The emergence of a more disciplinarist wing of the Reformed tradition—sharing Zurich's concern for biblical law and moral reform, but convinced that church authorities must energetically put these into practice through discipline—represented a delicate balancing act between Luther's original emphases and Anabaptist concerns for purity. This wing, consisting of leaders such as Johannes Oecolampadius, Martin Bucer, and above all John Calvin, maintained in principle the priesthood of all believers and the proclamatory, non-juridical essence of the church, but found it necessary to give a much larger role to clerically-overseen church discipline. This was in part a response to the demands of Anabaptists for a more visibly pure body of believers, in part the natural development of a new stress on sanctification as well as justification.[15] While none of these reformers denied Luther's insistence on the necessity of distinction between these two, and the absolute priority of justification, it seemed increasingly necessary, as evangelical doctrine took hold, to demand that faith bear good fruit among those professing Protestant doctrine. With this stress came a shifting accent in the doctrine of *adiaphora*: sanctification

---

[14] See for instance the excerpts from Martin Luther's *The Sermon on the Mount* in *From Irenaeus to Grotius*, ed. O'Donovan and O'Donovan, 595–602.

[15] Jordan Ballor and I explore these issues at more length in our essay, "European Calvinism: Church Discipline," in *European History Online* (EGO), ed. Irene Dingel and Johannes Paulmann (Mainz: Institute of European History [IEG], 2013), http://www.ieg-ego.eu/en/threads/crossroads/religious-and-denominational-spaces/jordan-ballor-w-bradford-littlejohn-european-calvinism-church-discipline.

could not really be said to be "indifferent to salvation," and so nor could anything that contributed to it. Although Luther had never denied the "third use of the law," it was increasingly emphasized by these other reformers, who viewed Scripture as a rule to guide Christian conduct individually and corporately. Viewed from this perspective, the realm of *adiaphora* contracted, since those matters determined by Scripture could not really be considered indifferent, and the role of ministers, as teachers of Scripture, expanded to include the oversight and censure of morals.

It is not surprising then, that in Calvin, the man who most successfully integrated these new emphases into a theological synthesis and implemented them in a community's practice, VanDrunen and others have identified the advent of a new, more institutional form of two kingdoms theology. For Calvin and his heirs, it is contended, the "spiritual government" is now as comprehensive as Scripture itself, and being concerned with outward order and behavior, must have outward mediators and rulers, independent from the civil government. If so, however, the doctrine of Christian liberty would seem to be in peril, since now it would appear that the conscience is in fact subject to human mediators within the spiritual kingdom of the church.

JOHN CALVIN'S TWO-KINGDOMS DOCTRINE

Calvin is also an obvious place to seek a two-kingdoms doctrine, because, unlike some other second-generation Reformers, we do not have to read between the lines to find it in his work. On the contrary, he is far less ambiguous even than Luther in setting it out at the center of his theology, inviting the question of why Calvin studies largely ignored the theme until David VanDrunen recently shined a spotlight on it. The doctrine appears in the all-important chapter III.19 of the *Institutes*, as Calvin concludes his discussion of justification and prepares to transition to his massive Bk. IV, entitled "The External Means or Aids By Which God Invites Us Into the Society of Christ and Holds Us Therein." Inasmuch as Calvin scholarship has attended at all to his two-kingdoms idea, it has frequently assumed, as VanDrunen does, that in delineating the "two kingdoms," Calvin intends to delineate the two distinct institutions within this sphere of external means—church and state. However, from a structural standpoint, it is more compelling to see his distinction of the two in III.19 as a center-post, with the "spiritual government" pointing back to his discussion of the inward reception of the grace of Christ in Book III, and the "temporal government" pointing forward to his discussion of the external means in Bk. IV—on this basis, both the visibly-organized church and the state would constitute external means in the temporal kingdom. Certainly Calvin's word choice in describing the two seems to bear out such a reading:

> The former [the spiritual government] has its seat within the soul, the latter [the temporal government] only regulates the external conduct. We may call the one the spiritual, the other the civil kingdom. Now, these two, as we have divided them, are always to be viewed apart from each other. When the one is considered, we should call off our minds, and not allow them to think of the other. For

> there exists in man a kind of two worlds, over which different kings and different laws can preside....The question...though not very obscure, or perplexing in itself, occasions difficulty to many, because they do not distinguish with sufficient accuracy between what is called the external forum, and the forum of conscience.[16]

The clear emphasis on "external" vs. "internal" seems a rather clear clue that Calvin is not, strictly speaking, discussing the spiritual kingdom in his discussion of the "external means" of ecclesiastical polity in Bk. IV. VanDrunen, however, does not pick up on this clue, and feels the need to chide Calvin for all his talk of "external" vs. "internal"—doesn't he realize that the Church and its ministry too are external? "Calvin surely did not mean to suggest that the spiritual kingdom is concerned only about things that are immaterial," he protests;[17] but it seems Calvin meant just this, writing in his *Commentary on 1 Corinthians*, "Christ's spiritual kingdom...has nothing to do with the body, and has nothing to do with the outward relationships of mankind, but has to do solely with the mind."[18]

---

[16] John Calvin, *Institutes of the Christian Religion*, ed. John T. McNeill, and trans. Ford Lewis Battles (Louisville: Westminster John Knox Press, 1960), III.19.15 (1:847).

[17] *Natural Law and the Two Kingdoms*, 91.

[18] Commentary on 1 Cor. 11:3 in *Commentary on the Epistles of Paul the Apostle to the Corinthians*, trans. John Pringle, 2 vols. (Edinburgh: Calvin Translation Society, 1848–49), 1:354.

In all this, Calvin certainly appears close to what we have seen of Luther.[19] Like Luther, too, Calvin developed his doctrine of the two kingdoms in close conjunction with his understanding of Christian liberty. Calvin calls Christian liberty "a thing of prime necessity," apart from which "consciences dare undertake almost nothing without doubting." Indeed, the doctrine is an "appendage of justification and is of no little avail in understanding its power."[20] As for Luther, this was not Christian liberty in the sense we often mean it today—the freedom of individual believers to act as they wish in matters where Scripture is silent—but is fundamentally soteriological, the proclamation of the freedom of the believer's conscience from the bondage of external works.

Calvin expounds three different elements to the doctrine:

> The first: that the consciences of believers, in seeking assurance of their justification before God, should rise above and advance beyond the law, forgetting all law righteousness....

> The second part, dependent upon the first, is that consciences observe the law, not as if constrained by the necessity of the law, but that freed from the law's yoke they willingly obey God's will. For since they dwell in per-

---

[19] A well-nuanced exposition of Calvin's two-kingdoms doctrine, highlighting his basic continuities with Luther as well as distinctive trajectories, has finally appeared in the form of Matthew J. Tuininga's *Calvin's Political Theology and the Public Engagement of the Church: Christ's Two Kingdoms* (Cambridge: Cambridge University Press, 2017).

[20] *Institutes* III.19.1 (1:833).

petual dread so long as they remain under the sway of the law, they will never be disposed with eager readiness to obey God unless they have already been given this sort of freedom....

The third part of Christian freedom lies in this: regarding outward things that are of themselves "indifferent" [*adiaphora*], we are not bound before God by any religious obligation preventing us from sometimes using them and other times not using them, indifferently.[21]

The last of these three, although the least important for Calvin, was to become the thorniest as the sixteenth century wore on, and is sometimes misunderstood by modern commentators, who fail to grasp the stress on "religious obligation," and miss Calvin's reminder, "that Christian freedom is, in all its parts a spiritual thing. Its whole force of consists in quieting frightened consciences before God."[22] If we do not attend to this line, we might think that Calvin here means to say that human authorities cannot prescribe outward conduct for believers in matters indifferent, without abridging Christian liberty. Obviously, taken without qualification, this would overthrow all human government, since civil magistrates must frequently pass laws regarding things otherwise indifferent. David VanDrunen, then, assumes that Calvin must here mean this limitation to apply only within the church, with civil

---

[21] *Institutes* III.19.2, 4, 7 (1:834, 836, 838).

[22] *Institutes* III.19.9 (1:840).

magistrates free to limit Christian liberty. In fact, he takes this limitation to be the foundation of Calvin's two-kingdoms distinction:

> In the spiritual kingdom of the church, eccle-siastical authorities, dealing only with spiritual things, have no power to bind consciences beyond the declaration of what Scripture itself teaches (a 'ministerial' authority) and believers have no conscientious obligation to believe or do anything that the church says otherwise. Believers are free from anything 'beside' the word of God. In the civil kingdom and with respect to civil matters, however, believers are free only from commands 'contrary' to Scrip-ture, meaning that they are conscientiously bound to do all things that the magistrate commands (however disagreeable) so long as they do not contradict some biblical teach-ing.[23]

By this means, VanDrunen arrives at the idea, which has influenced much of the recent revival of two-kingdoms doctrine, that the two kingdoms are, roughly speaking, "church" and "state."

It is the case that Calvin introduces his doctrine of the two kingdoms in this context, but he does so precisely to prevent this sort of confusion. In fact, immediately before introducing it, he asserts unequivocally that, according to the doctrine of Christian liberty, "we conclude that they [believers' consciences] are released

---

[23] *Natural Law and the Two Kingdoms*, 191.

from the power of *all men*"[24]—clearly including civil authority—but then immediately going on to stress that this does not do away with human authority, for he is talking about the inward forum of *conscience*, not the external forum of action. Confusion only arises, he says, when we "do not sharply enough distinguish the outer forum, as it is called, and the forum of the conscience." So he defines conscience for us: "it is a certain mean between God and man...[an] awareness which hales man before God's judgment."[25]

> Therefore, as works have regard to men, so conscience refers to God. A good conscience, then, is nothing but inward integrity of heart....Properly speaking, as I have already said, it has respect to God alone....Hence it comes about that a law is said to bind the conscience when it simply binds a man without regard to other men, or without taking them into account.[26]

Human laws, whether civil or ecclesiastical, are directed toward the horizontal dimension of human action, that which concerns other men, and hence belong to the civil kingdom. Thus, when Calvin says that Christian liberty means that we cannot be bound by a "religious obligation" in things indifferent, he means that quite precisely; laws could and often should be imposed for order, decorum, and edification, both in church and in

---

[24] *Institutes* III.19.14 (1:846); emphasis mine.

[25] *Institutes* III.19.15 (1:848).

[26] *Institutes* III.19.16 (1:849).

state. Indeed, given the non-spiritual nature (in this precise sense of spiritual) of most ecclesiastical laws, Calvin saw no reason to make them the domain of church authorities alone, but gave magistrates in Geneva an important role in matters of worship and church order.[27] In all this, Calvin's approach to the two-kingdoms was substantially the same as Luther's.

[27] See Tuininga, *Calvin's Political Theology*, 223–24.

III:
THE TWO KINGDOMS
FROM CALVIN TO HOOKER

CHURCH DISCIPLINE AND THE TWO KINGDOMS

DESPITE the basic continuities between Calvin's formulation of the two kingdoms and that of Luther, there were some emergent differences in Calvin's thought and practice that helped shape a different understanding of the doctrine within some branches of the Reformed tradition (including that to which VanDrunen has recently given voice). Although Calvin never changed his crucial discussion of Christian liberty and the two kingdoms in the *Institutes* on from what he penned in the original 1535 edition, he did develop new emphases that were to create some tensions. In particular, Calvin greatly expanded his section on the visible church in Bk. IV, and emphasized more and more the God-ordained character of its external means as the necessary channels through which Christ spiritually governs his church. The office of clergy as "spiritual governors" was accentuated, as was the close Scriptural regulation of church order. This shift chiefly focused on Calvin's understanding of church discipline.

Church discipline occupied a murky middle ground between the two kingdoms (as evidenced by the equivocation of many sixteenth-century theologians and confessions on whether it should be considered a third mark of the church or not). After all, it is a pronouncement about the hidden internal forum (whether or not a conscience is right with God) that must take effect in the visible external forum (removing a congregant from the eucharistic assembly); its power consists purely in the declarative power of the Word, but it requires a certain coercive imposition in the here and now. For Calvin, its importance in the life of the church was too great for it to be left to mere laymen. Accordingly, although lay-elders joined with ministers in making decisions about church discipline on Geneva's Consistory, and although most Genevan lay-elders were magistrates on the City Council, Calvin insisted that they exercised church discipline *only* in their role as church officers, rather than civil officers. After all, although the civil polity was rightly concerned, in Calvin's eyes, with godly religious practice as well as with public morality and order, there was a difference between sins and crimes, and between what church discipline and civil justice aimed to achieve. Thus there emerged a clear distinction between civil and ecclesiastical rule in Calvin's Geneva, with the latter straddling the barrier between the hidden spiritual kingdom and the outward civil kingdom.[1]

---

[1] For a good overview of the vision for church discipline in Calvin's Geneva and the tensions surrounding it, see Robert M. Kingdon, "Social Control and Political Control in Calvin's Geneva," in *Die Reformation in Deutschland und Europa: Interpretationen und Debatten*, ed. Hans. R. Guggisberg and Gottfried G. Krodel (Gütersloh: Gütersloher Verlagshaus, 1993), 521–32; Gillian Lewis, "Calvinism in Geneva in the Time of Calvin and of Beza (1541–1605)," in *International Calvinism,*

Other Reformed polities, taking their lead more from Zurich, laid more stress on the essentially external character of church discipline as the regulation of good behavior in the community, and accordingly treated it as a largely civil matter, under the jurisdiction of laymen in the church in their capacity of magistrates. Thomas Erastus in Heidelberg argued particularly strenuously for this position, considering Calvin's scheme at risk of resurrecting the papal tyranny of a twofold coercive jurisdiction over believers. Disagreement between these two approaches was to persist in Switzerland, Germany, the Netherlands, and England for many decades. Both, however, shared a Christendom model of the church and society, considering these terms to be the same community viewed from two different perspectives. Accordingly, the distinction between civil and ecclesiastical functions did not entail a reconception of the two kingdoms as primarily an institutional separation, and certainly not one characterized by a modern "sacred" vs. "secular" distinction. Again, Calvin himself never doubted that the external care for the church fell within the limits of civil jurisdiction, declaring that it was "to cherish and protect the outward worship of God, to defend sound doctrine of piety and the position of the Church."[2] As with Luther, however, this rule was executed according to principles of natural equity, not divine law, and in principle, the magistrates ruled according to their discretion, not the dictates of the clergy (although in practice, this was not always the case in

---

1541–1715, ed. Menna Prestwich (Oxford: Oxford University Press, 1985), 39–70.

[2] Calvin, *Institutes*, IV.20.2 (2:1487).

Geneva). The exercise of human authority, whether in church and state, remained—although tenuously—an exercise of prudence and charity in the government of things indifferent, not the voice of God.

THE ROLE OF *JURE DIVINO* PRESBYTERIANISM

A shift toward a more institutional understanding of the two kingdoms can be seen among some in the Reformed tradition by the later sixteenth century. In this shift, the emergence of *jure divino* presbyterianism (the view that Scripture strictly required presbyterian church government) played a significant role. Given the close connection of the two-kingdoms doctrine to the doctrine of Christian liberty, it should not be hard to see why. If the Word of God has strictly required a particular system of church government, then implementation of it is binding on conscience and such government no longer falls within the realm of prudence that characterized the Reformers' understanding of the civil kingdom. Moreover, if the officers of that government speak directly for God (as in some understandings of *jure divino*) then all that they ordain would seem to belong to the spiritual kingdom. After all, the civil kingdom was defined by Luther and Calvin at one where God's rule is mediated only *indirectly* through human authorities, who could not therefore bind the conscience.

Calvin's successor Theodore Beza at Geneva is sometimes identified as the source of this shift, and certainly he did go further than Calvin in asserting a biblical requirement for presbyterianism, and the authority of ministers.[3]

---

[3] See Tadataka Maruyama, *The Ecclesiology of Theodore Beza: The Reform of the True Church* (Geneva: Librairie Droz, 1978).

However, the close cooperation of ministry and magistracy in Geneva tempered any move to externalize the spiritual kingdom as a separate institution. By the same token, however, the deep conflicts that emerged between magistracy and ministry in Elizabethan England encouraged such a development, particularly among the Puritans.

Queen Elizabeth's Protestant bishops had defended her authority to enforce uniformity in various ecclesiastical ceremonies, as matters purely external, and contended that this posed no problem for Christian liberty in the spiritual kingdom of conscience, since no doctrinal claims were being made about the ceremonies. But for many English Protestants, the ceremonies did pose a problem of conscience, as they seemed inherently superstitious or popish. The intense pressures of conscience created by this tension between loyalty to the Queen and concern over superstition bred a series of rapid shifts in the 1560s and 1570s. First, the very notion of *adiaphora* was seriously questioned, as the emerging Puritans asked whether God would really have left the Church without guidance on such important questions; if Scripture was really the rule for Christian life, did it not provide detailed guidance for all matters of church order? At the same time, the bishops became the scapegoats for the lack of adequate reforms and the radical Cambridge theologian Thomas Cartwright advanced the theory that bishops were unbiblical and God required Presbyterian church government. Although not explicitly renouncing the Queen's authority over the church, he advanced the idea that the church, conceived in terms of the ordained clergy, could autonomously govern its own affairs—a concept derived partly from Beza, but even more so from the paradigm of the "stranger churches," which many English Protestants had experienced during their exile under Bloody Mary. Such an independent body, moreover, could ensure a much purer and more disciplined membership than the "mixed multitude" of the national Protestant churches—in short, the visible church could approximate the invisible.[4]

Taken together, these concepts—a detailed Scriptural blueprint for the church, Presbyterian ministers as the authorized interpreters of the same, and the ideal of a pure and disciplined body of "visible saints"—provided the building blocks for a new mutation of the two-kingdoms doctrine. In England, this received its fullest expression in the works of Thomas Cartwright and Walter Travers in the 1570s and 1580s, although Andrew Melville was simultaneously advancing a similar paradigm in Scotland, where it would leave a lasting stamp. For these men the two kingdoms represent two external manifestations of God's rule—the one through ministers and their disciplinary regime; the other through magistrates and their disciplinary regime. Each presided over a distinct society with distinct ends and strictly defined responsibilities.

The implications for political theology were dramatic, threatening to upset the delicate balance in Protestant political theology between the magistrate's secular (as an officer of the temporal kingdom ruling by human law) and sacred (as a principle member of the church charged with the care of the same) roles. Many modern writers have hailed the Puritan project as a campaign for religious liberty that anticipated later separations of church and

---

[4] For a fuller exposition of these themes, see ch. 3 of my *Peril and Promise of Christian Liberty.*

state.[5] However, for all the genuinely great achievements of Puritanism, religious liberty was not one of them. To be sure, the separatist wing of Puritanism did aim at a kind of separation of church and state, but only so that it was free to impose strict religious authority within the separated community. Most Puritans, meanwhile, sought to dictate the terms of reformation for the national established church according to what they took to be the commands of Scripture, allowing very little room for dissent. The fractious sectarianism that resulted when both parties made their way to the Massachusetts Bay Colony was a natural result of trying too hard to make the spiritual kingdom of Christ take visible shape in a pure and sanctified human community.[6] Indeed, their conformist opponents in England charged that Puritan clericalism reproduced the evils of high medieval papalism, in which the magistrate was bound to frame his laws according to clerical dictates, and enforce their policies. By dramatically shrinking the realm of *adiaphora*, Puritanism rolled back key gains of the Reformation; believers' consciences once again had to tread carefully around a thicket of moral and ecclesiastical regulations, fearful that any transgression was rebellion against God.

It was thus—paradoxically to our ears—in *defense* of Christian liberty that English theology Richard Hooker took up his pen to justify the magistrate's authority to impose religious uniformity.

---

[5] See for instance Douglas F. Kelly, *The Emergence of Liberty in the Modern World: The Influence of Calvin on Five Governments From the 16th Through 18th Centuries* (Phillipsburg, NJ: P&R Publishing, 1992).

[6] See Michael P. Winship, *Godly Republicanism: Puritans, Pilgrims, and a City on a Hill* (Cambridge, MA: Harvard University Press, 2012).

RICHARD HOOKER'S APPROACH TO "THINGS INDIFFERENT"

Few figures in the history of theology can boast as contested a legacy as Richard Hooker, the purported forefather of a protean *via media* that is redefined with dizzying frequency. Until recently, many readings of Hooker suffered from the insularity that characterized much of Anglican historiography, doggedly committed to the assumption that England had its own history, blissfully independent from goings-on on the Continent. So when historian Torrance Kirby suggested that in fact, Richard Hooker should be read as a theologian of the magisterial Reformation, he touched a raw nerve among Hooker scholars, generating a hostile backlash that, after two decades, shows no sign of letting up.[7] Perhaps tellingly, none of the responses to Kirby and his followers has bothered to engage the thesis at the heart of his reinterpretation, that Hooker's theological response to Puritanism rested throughout on his Protestant—indeed, Lutheran—two-kingdoms doctrine.

Given the prominence of the doctrine in earlier conformist/Puritan polemics, it is no surprise that we should find Hooker relying on it in his magisterial defense of the Church of England, *The Lawes of Ecclesiasticall Politie*. However, it would be a mistake to imagine that Hooker is

---

[7] Kirby ignited the dispute with his 1990 *Richard Hooker's Doctrine of the Royal Supremacy* (Leiden: Brill, 1990). For an overview of the conflict since, see my "Search for a Reformed Hooker," *Reformation & Renaissance Review* 16, no. 1 (2014): 68–82. For the latest attempt to grapple in depth with these questions, see W. Bradford Littlejohn and Scott N. Kindred-Barnes, eds., *Richard Hooker and Reformed Orthodoxy* (Göttingen: Vandenhoeck and Ruprecht, 2017).

merely re-stating the consensus teaching of the Tudor church. On the contrary, although the paradigm of the two kingdoms had been frequently invoked by his predecessors, it was bedeviled by significant tensions, in at least two respects.

First, his predecessors, while saying that the sphere of the magistrate's authority in the church was only over "things indifferent," not over the substance of faith or the ministry of word and sacraments, had a tendency to say that this authority itself was not a thing indifferent. Rather, the royal supremacy over the church was grounded on divine law; it was the model God had established in the Old Testament, and Christian polities had no right to alter it. If a key feat of Luther's two kingdoms doctrine had been to desacralize earthly kingship, and indeed all human rule, some Elizabethan Protestants who invoked the doctrine clearly didn't get the memo. In texts such as Bishop Jewel's classic *Apology of the Church of England* (1563), the idea of sacred kingship was alive and well.[8] To this extent there was some justice in the complaint that the Tudors merely substituted the prince for the Pope— although certainly such apologists held firmly to the crucial two-kingdoms idea that the prince had no authority over conscience.

Their tension here was part of a larger ambiguity that vexed Protestant discussions of *adiaphora*—was this category defined by all those things "not necessary to salvation" or those things "not commanded or forbidden in Scripture"? Things "indifferent" in the first sense might

---

[8] Andre A. Gazal, *Scripture and Royal Supremacy in Tudor England: The Use of Old Testament Historical Narrative* (Lewiston: Edwin Mellen Press, 2013).

well not be in the second sense, and this equivocation began to confuse discussions considerably, particularly as Puritans began to insist, in a very un-Lutheran turn, that obedience to all God's Biblical commands was in some sense necessary to salvation.[9] In critiquing Puritanism, then, Hooker also set himself the task of sorting out the conformist case. He clarified the relation of these different senses of *adiaphora*, and decisively undermining the idea of sacred kingship by rooting the royal supremacy squarely in the soil of natural and human law, rather than divine law.

Indeed, he famously begins the *Lawes of Ecclesiasticall Politie* with a masterful disquisition on the various forms of law, their relation to each other, and their relation to the one eternal law in the bosom of God within which they all find their unity and common *telos*. In this account, which constituted an influential revival of Protestant Thomism, Hooker classifies human law, which governs all "politique societies," as the product of rational discernment of the natural law (or what Hooker calls the "law of reason") and its application by an act of corporate will (legislation) upon a body politic. Supernatural, or divine law is not to be understood as everything in Scripture—everything that is supernatural in respect of origin—but rather as that which is supernatural in respect of its end. In other words, the supernatural law is that which directs us to our end of union with God of which sin has made us utterly

---

[9] As Thomas Cartwright put it, unless we "have the word of God go before us in all our actions ... we cannot otherwise be assured that they please God" (*The Second Replie of Thomas Cartwright: Agaynst Master Doctor Whitgifts Second Answer Touching the Church Discipline* [Heidelberg: 1575], 61). For further exposition of this theme, see Stephen Brachlow, *The Communion of Saints: Radical Puritan and Separatist Ecclesiology, 1570–1625* (Oxford: Oxford University Press, 1988), ch. 3.

incapable, it establishes the way of salvation; in short, it governs the spiritual kingdom.[10]

But what does Hooker do with the fact that so much of Scripture talks about things besides the way of salvation, about matters of the civil kingdom—that is, how does he resolve the discontinuity between the two senses of *adiaphora*? His answer of course is that the divine law of Scripture contains not merely the supernatural law, but restates much of the content of natural law, as well as offering by example many human law applications of natural law. Why? Because Hooker, as a good Protestant, understands that fallen reason is very prone to go astray even in earthly matters, and will profit greatly from this clearer teaching. However, Hooker insists that Scripture is here restating and clarifying something in the moral law that is already binding—it is already normative by virtue of creation, not by virtue of Scripture. The same, crucially, is true for human law, and this is at the core of his response to both Puritans and over-enthusiastic conformists. If a law contained in Scripture has, formally, the character of human law—that is to say, positive law which applies the principles of the natural law to the changeable needs of human polities—then the fact that it is contained in Scripture does not change this status. So, for instance, inasmuch as our circumstances remain the same as those of ancient Israel or the New Testament church, the positive laws there established, as infallible (because given

---

[10] Hooker's main exposition of these distinctions can be found in Book I of his *Lawes of Ecclesiastical Politie*, which will be shortly be appearing in a modern English "translation": W. Bradford Littlejohn, Brian Marr, and Bradley Belschner, eds., *A Christian Theory of Law: A Modernization of Book I of Richard Hooker's Laws of Ecclesiastical Polity* (Moscow, ID: The Davenant Press, 2017).

in Scripture) descriptions of what natural law required then, still bind us. But if our circumstances have changed, we are free to use reason, illuminated by attention to Scriptural principles and precedents, to do otherwise.[11]

The mention of the "New Testament church" highlights the fact that for Hooker, when we are talking about "human law" we are not talking only about strictly civil law. This is where his two-kingdoms doctrine plays a key role. The church, he insists, exists in two aspects: invisibly, as a perfect body of the redeemed, before God, and visibly, as a mixed community of professing Christians, before the world. In its latter identity, the church is a "politic society," requiring rule, authority, and public order like any other. As such, it is governed by human law, which may be derived from natural law.[12] However highly we esteem the authority of Scripture then, says Hooker, there is thus no reason why we should expect to find detailed regulations of church order in Scripture—as we do not in fact, contrary to earnest Puritan attempts to find them. Even where we do find such regulations, they are subject to the proviso about changing circumstances— they may or may not still be binding in detail for church polity and liturgy. Accordingly, it is because, in Protestant England, the company of professing believers is coterminous with the commonwealth, that the head of state may legitimately exercise supreme juridical authority over matters of church polity. This need not always be the

---

[11] Hooker, *Lawes*, I.15, http://oll.libertyfund.org/titles/hooker-the-works-of-richard-hooker-vol-1.

[12] Hooker, *Lawes*, III.1-3, 9-11, http://oll.libertyfund.org/titles/hooker-the-works-of-richard-hooker-vol-1. For a fuller exposition, see my *Peril and Promise*, ch. 4.

case—although Hooker believes that Christian rulers should always be concerned for the protection and advancement of true religion in their realms—but it is an eminently reasonable and Scripturally defensible arrangement under the conditions pertaining in Elizabethan England.[13]

HOOKER'S TWO-KINGDOM DOCTRINE

On the matter of the two kingdoms itself, Hooker recognized that there had indeed been a pervasive ambiguity within the magisterial Protestant formulation, which had left room for Puritans like Thomas Cartwright to re-conceptualize the two kingdoms in institutional terms. Cartwright, like VanDrunen and many modern advocates of the two-kingdoms doctrine, asks whether it really makes sense to distinguish the spiritual and temporal kingdoms as "internal" and "external." After all, is not the church concerned fundamentally with spiritual matters, under the headship of Christ? And are not these matters attended to by human ministers, working outwardly and visibly in their preaching and administration of the sacraments? Is not such external ministry still spiritual and thus totally distinct from the laws and regulations that are the concern of the civil magistrate in the temporal kingdom?

Hooker offers to clear up the confusion by granting that we may indeed use the word "spiritual" in this broader

---

[13] Hooker, *Lawes* VIII.3, http://oll.libertyfund.org/titles/hooker-the-works-of-richard-hooker-vol-3. For a fuller exposition, see my *Peril and Promise*, ch. 6.

sense, so long as we retain a clear distinction between Christ's inward work and the outward work of the church:

> To make things therefore so plain that hence-forth a child's capacity may serve rightly to conceive our meaning: we make the spiritual regiment of Christ to be generally that where-by his Church is ruled and governed in things spiritual. Of this general we make two distinct kinds; the one invisibly exercised by Christ himself in his own person, the other outward-ly administered by them whom Christ doth allow to be the Rulers and guides of his Church.

> Touching the former of these two kinds, we teach that Christ in regard thereof is particu-larly termed the Head of the Church of God; neither can any other creature in that sense and meaning be termed head besides him, be-cause it importeth the conduct and govern-ment of our souls, by the hand of that blessed Spirit wherewith we are sealed and marked, as being peculiarly his. Him only therefore we do acknowledge to be that Lord, which dwelleth, liveth, and reigneth in our hearts; him only to be that Head, which giveth life and salvation unto his body; him only to be that fountain, from whence the influence of heavenly grace distilleth, and is derived into all parts, whether the word, or sacraments, or discipline, or whatsoever be the mean whereby it floweth.

The outward ministry of the Church, however, "is indeed both Spiritual and His. . . howbeit neither spiritual, as that which is inwardly and invisibly exercised; nor His, as that which He Himself in person doth exercise." Moreover, although the main part of this ministry belongs to the clergy alone, Hooker argues that we may further distinguish the "power of dominion," of ruling over the outward structure of the church, which is, to be sure, still "spiritual" in the sense of being concerned with spiritual things, but temporal in the mode of its administration, and thus subject to prudential deliberation.[14]

Hooker complements this picture with what we might call his doctrine of correspondences, his insistence that the church outwardly ought to seek to correspond to its inward reality. "Signs must resemble the things they signify," he declares, and we might legitimately speak of the visible church, in his theology, as a sign which signifies the presence of the invisible. Accordingly, it must strive to manifest outwardly the qualities which it has antecedently in Christ:

> That which inwardly each man should be, the Church outwardly ought to testify. And therefore the duties of our religion which are seen must be such as that affection which is unseen ought to be. Signs must resemble the things they signify. If religion bear the greatest sway in our hearts, our outward religious duties must show it, as far as the Church hath

---

[14] Hooker, *Lawes* VIII.4.10, http://oll.libertyfund.org/titles/hooker-the-works-of-richard-hooker-vol-3 (note that in the newer critical editions, the section numbers have changed and this is now VIII.4.9).

outward ability....Yea, then are the public duties of religion best ordered, when the militant Church doth resemble by sensible means, as it may in such cases, the hidden dignity and glory wherewith the Church triumphant in heaven is beautified.[15]

The clear distinction between the two kingdoms, then, is no license for apathy about the visible and temporal ordering of the Christian community, especially as it is gathered for worship in the church. We can and must seek for the visible church to reflect and point us to the invisible, but as a sign or sacrament, not the thing itself.

We can now see why Hooker's *Lawes* represents such an important contribution to Protestant two-kingdoms theology, even if we might resist the conclusions Hooker himself draws for religious uniformity and royal supremacy. However oppressive these might seem to us today, they were, at least as understood and defended by Hooker, much less so than the Puritan legalism he opposed, which brooked no opposition and left no room for discretion in the outward ordering of the Christian community. Hooker deserves credit for freeing Christian consciences from the tyranny of Scripture conceived as an exhaustive law-book, desacralizing human authority in both church and state, and resisting the Puritan tendency to immanentize Christ's eschatological rule in the visible church. In all this he both

---

[15] Hooker, *Lawes*, V.6.1-2, http://oll.libertyfund.org/titles/hooker-the-works-of-richard-hooker-vol-2. For a fuller exposition, see chs. 10-11 of my *Richard Hooker: A Companion to His Life and Work* (Eugene, OR: Cascade, 2015).

re-affirmed the core agenda of Luther's reform, but he also clarified and filled out Luther's sometimes paradoxical formulations by spelling out how it was that the visible church had a foot in both kingdoms, so to speak.

IV:
CONTRIBUTIONS OF TWO-KINGDOMS THOUGHT

THE REJECTION OF IDOLATRY

AT ITS most basic, the two-kingdoms doctrine was the Reformation's rebuke to idolatry—to the idolatries of the Church of Rome in particular, but in principle to any that the human heart, that "factory of idols," as Calvin called it, could produce. The two-kingdoms doctrine was a rebuke to our eagerness to call Christ down from heaven, seeing his hand in our own works and hearing his voice in our own words. It was an eschatological reminder that we live in a time between the times of Christ's coming, that regardless of our duty to witness to the reign of the Son of Man, that reign remains hidden behind the "masks" that God has ordained to do his will in history.

Concretely in the sixteenth century, this rejection of idolatry made itself felt in nearly area of life which the medieval church had colonized: icons and relics that were seen as conduits to heaven were tossed out, sacraments and rituals that had been granted the power to unite to Christ were understood instead as mere instruments for faith to do its mighty work, and the exaltation of clerical and monastic life as a unique participation in the heavenly kingdom was rejected in favor of the priesthood of all believers. But most importantly, the Reformers questioned the idolatrous framework of authority claimed by the late medieval church, and this was where the two-kingdoms doctrine did its most important work. Neither the Pope nor any of his henchmen could claim coercive temporal authority within Christendom, nor any exemption from the appropriate temporal authority exercised by magistrates. Within the spiritual realm, church ministers did still exercise an important authority, but one that was purely declarative, and thoroughly fallible. Christ alone reigned over the hearts of believers, such that no hypocrite could find a place in his kingdom however many priests he might impress, and no repentant sinner would find heaven's door shut against him, whatever sentences of excommunication stood in the way.

Of course, since the Reformers rightly insisted that there is still such a thing as an ordained ministry, gifted with a unique authority to proclaim the Word and protect the church, they did not always find it easy to maintain the full force of their revolution. Creatures of sense that we are, the invisibility of the church naturally makes us nervous, and it should be no surprise that in the sixteenth century and beyond, various Protestant ecclesiologies often fell afoul of the two-kingdoms doctrine, whether through Anabaptistic sects that stressed too much the purity of the body, or high church presbyterians or episcopalians who insisted that God's grace could only flow through properly authorized ecclesiastical structures. Even in low-church America, Protestantism has produced a steady stream of sects, cults, and personality-driven institutions that have dangerously conflated a particular institution with the kingdom of Christ. Still, the accomplishment of the Reformation in reconceptualizing the church has been real and lasting.

THE CHANGING ROLE OF THE STATE

The profound demystification of clerical authority achieved by the Reformation meant the corresponding empowerment of lay authority in church and society. To this extent, the Reformation has been cynically seen as the long-awaited victory of secular rulers over churchmen in the late medieval struggle between church and state. Indeed, many have lamented the Reformation's reconfiguration of authority within Christendom, seeing in it the seedbeds of a statist absolutism no better than (or perhaps considerably worse than, depending on the commentator) papist absolutism. Was not the Reformation responsible, we are asked, for the rise of divine-right absolutist monarchies and despotic nation-states in the seventeenth century, and, in due course, of nationalist idolatries and atrocities in the nineteenth and twentieth centuries?

There is no question that the retreat of the old church left cunning civil authorities space to consolidate their powers to an unprecedented extent in the early modern period, for both good and ill, nor that the two kingdoms doctrine itself was sometimes used to justify despotic ideas (as in Thomas Hobbes's *Leviathan*). However, the overall tendency of Protestantism was to undermine the theological foundations of absolutism in state as well as church. For whereas medieval monarchs had found a place within the web of sacral hierarchy that structured late medieval society, the two-kingdoms theory de-sacralized, or more properly, de-totalized, the State and the exercise of civil authority. Political authority was still ordained by God, accountable to God, and indeed redeemed in Christ, to be sure, and to this extent, could be said to mediate his rule. However, this rule of God's "left hand" was radically distinct from His proper work of redemption and oversaw matters of temporary and limited significance; civil authorities were responsible to preserve the created order, not to bring in the new creation. This teaching set a decisive limit to the scope of civil authority, or the sorts of demands it could make. Of course, medieval papalism had certainly limited the state as well, but by seeking to make the civil authorities the policemen of the church, it had made rulers tangle matters of conscience with politics, making heresy a civil crime. Although haltingly and inconsistently, Luther's heirs worked to disentangle these two. Indeed, it is perhaps worth noting that although divine right absolutism made some headway in Protestant England in the seventeenth century (notably with Charles I), it proved short-lived and self-defeating there at the same time that it was putting down deep and lasting roots in Catholic France.

Moreover, although there is a live debate as to whether the early modern period saw an increase in war and violence in western Europe, the justification for violence was dramatically scaled back by the Reformation. Luther's two-kingdoms theory radically de-sacralized violence, associating it entirely with temporal rule and very limited temporal ends, and many of his heirs admirably carried forward this legacy.[1]

Of course, it is true that nature abhors a vacuum, and so it is no surprise that the mystique of sacred authority, having been dislodged from individual authorities in church and state, should attach itself to what, according to Luther, was the true priesthood: the whole Christian people. Nationalist movements in the nineteenth and twentieth century, with their tendency to sacralize the whole nation or people, could be seen as ripple effects of Protestant two-kingdoms doctrine, even if they could only succeed by ignoring its basic premise: a refusal to immanentize the eschaton, to attribute eschatological ultimacy to any earthly structure or community.

ENDURING RELEVANCE

Still, from our 21st-century viewpoint, we may ask whether this legacy of the Reformation might not have gone too far. Certainly, five hundred years ago, it may have been necessary to free the individual conscience from oppressive spiritual authorities, but today, the need is to convince individuals that they need to listen to spiritual authorities at all! The de-sacralization of institutions and human authorities has gone so far that for us today, nothing is sacred—nothing, that is, except the fleeting desires of the individual. A steady stream of modernity critics have lamented the "disenchantment" of the world wrought by

---

[1] For a good example of the impact of two-kingdoms political theology in helping to carve out space for religious liberty, see Eric Nelson, *The Hebrew Republic: : Jewish Sources and the Transformation of European Political Thought* (Cambridge, MA: Harvard University Press, 2010).

the Reformation, which led inexorably if unintentionally, they charge, to the dreary amoral world of modern secularism, in which God seems dead and man remakes the world at his own whim.

It is more than we can do here to properly engage these sweeping arguments, but it is worth pausing to consider the oddity of the charge that Protestantism drove God out of everyday life. After all, it was Luther's intention to do just the opposite—to bring Christianity out of the monasteries and private masses of the chantry chapels into the ordinary life of the layman. To be sure, hearing priests chant in a foreign language behind an altar screen may have induced a certain *frisson*, but the Lutheran farmer lustily singing psalms in German while he ploughed his fields surely had a fuller sense of the presence of God in his work and in the world. The magisterial Reformers sought to transform the notion of the "spiritual kingdom" from an institutional realm of the clergy alone to a dimension of existence animating every aspect of a Christian's life.

Those two-kingdoms advocates today who want to combat the disenchantment of modernity by reasserting the notion of the institutional church as spiritual kingdom are thus sadly mistaken. To be sure, we need to regain a sense of the objectivity of the means of grace experienced in corporate worship as the central wellspring which will flow out to every corner of our lives. And we need to renounce the triumphalistic transformationalism that seeks to make every field of Christian discipleship a form of kingdom-building, placing an inappropriate eschatological burden on the mundane tasks of trying to live out authentic humanity in a broken world. But it is no better to place an undue eschatological burden on the work of the visible church.

Accordingly, we will begin the second part of this guide, which seeks to put the two-kingdoms doctrine to work in the contemporary task of Christian discipleship, with a consideration of what two-kingdoms ecclesiology looks like today.

V:

TWO KINGDOMS IN THE CHURCH

AS I HAVE said in previous chapters, the doctrine of the two kingdoms is often misunderstood as a distinction between the church and something else—be it the state, civil society, or cultural life in general. In fact, the church itself lives in both kingdoms, and indeed nowhere is it more important to remember this eschatological distinction than when it comes to the work of the church. Precisely because the church is the sign of Christ's presence and reign in the world, it is tempting to mistake sign for reality, and place an unsustainable burden of expectations on an institution that remains, for all the glimmers of grace that shine through it, all too human. In this chapter, I will consider the value of a two-kingdoms ecclesiology from two main perspectives: first, how to understand the ministerial task of preaching, pastoring, and discipline; and second, what it means for the church to be a visible body, and how this relates to ecumenical aspirations.

TWO KINGDOMS PASTORING

It's tough being a pastor. I know because I've never dared try, but I've watched others try. Sure, you can always avoid preaching on anything so concrete and close to home as to ruffle any feathers, and some ministers have perfected the art of doing so for years on end. But as soon as he takes seriously his task as a shepherd of souls, the minister is likely to hear howls of indignation raised—he is a legalist, a killjoy, binding consciences and trampling on Christian liberty. Or perhaps, depending on his congregation, he may find himself accused of being a softie or an antinomian, refusing to man up and speak uncompromisingly to our culture. In the privacy of one-on-one counseling, he may not have a whole audience second-guessing him, but he will certainly second-guess himself: does this erring soul need to be comforted with the promises of the gospel, or jarred out of complacency with a reminder of God's judgment against sinners? One wrong move may be a matter of spiritual life and death.

Faced with this dilemma, many pastors, in conservative circles at least, make it their aim to "say nothing but what the Bible says." In one sense this is not only laudable but necessary: the Bible is the authoritative guide for both faith and practice, and the final standard for adjudicating any doctrinal question. And much of what the pastor is called to do is simply to proclaim the gospel. But the good news is, as Oliver O'Donovan has said, a "demanding comfort,"[1] and the task of pastoring means knowing how to apply both demand and comfort to the concrete lives of

---

[1] Oliver O'Donovan, *The Church in Crisis: The Gay Controversy and the Anglican Communion* (Eugene, OR: Cascade Books, 2008), 104.

his flock, which will necessarily take him beyond Scripture—if not its spirit, certainly its letter. To preach and pastor effectively, the minister must be waist-deep in the stuff of everyday life, the myriad personal, social, political, and cultural challenges that confront his congregation and that at every point draw them closer to or drag them further from the face of God. And Scripture, it must be said, does not address home mortgages or gay marriage or online pornography as such—*obviously*, it does address debt and sexuality and lust, but these specific challenges that confront us, in all their concrete particularity and novelty, are not in view in the biblical text.

"Saying nothing but what the Bible says," then, can take two forms. Either the minister, fearing to bind consciences beyond the Word by any specific application, avoids as much as possible in the pulpit the pressing social and cultural concerns of the day with which his congregation wrestles the other six days of the week, and confines himself primarily to theological lectures in lieu of sermons, or to vague platitudes when it comes to ethical matters. Or else the minister, convinced that the Bible really *does* speak to everything, proceeds to read the concerns of the day— gun control, home mortgages, or healthcare policy— straight into the biblical text, closing with a thunderous "Thus saith the Lord!" (Presumably all those who disagree with the application are blinded by sin.) In pastoral counseling, "the Bible only" has often come to mean something like the "nouthetic counseling" approach, in which the complexities of human psychology and the details of particular circumstances are all filtered out and the struggling soul is told only "confess and repent of your rebellion against God." All this in the name of protecting Christian liberty.

For advocates of modern R2K doctrine, one of the important reasons for the two-kingdoms distinction is to preserve Christian liberty from such pulpit-bullying. And they are quite right in this concern; indeed, for Luther and Calvin, as we've already seen, a chief purpose of the doctrine was to prevent clergy from inappropriately binding the consciences of the laity. However, we should not imagine that by simply distinguishing political matters as "civil kingdom," off-limits for pastors, we will have solved the problem. To be sure, great political and social questions add a whole new level of complexity which makes it difficult to bring Scripture directly to bear on them. But even if the pastor studiously avoids offering any guidance on political questions, the problem remains. For no man is an island, and our sins generally have a social and cultural dimension. In other words, they are the complex interplay of what flows from our wicked hearts and what we encounter in and imbibe from the world around us. This milieu, again, differs in key ways from ancient Israel or first-century Palestine, and the pastor will have to rely on a well-informed judgment of his context, and a well-developed sense of prudence, if he is to rightly apply the Word to the lives of his flock. If "Christian liberty" or the division of the "two kingdoms" restricts the pastor from ever speaking beyond the words of Scripture, then clearly it will restrict him from a large part of what it really means to pastor.

Perhaps the solution to this dilemma is to recognize that the pastor himself has a foot in both kingdoms, and I don't just mean in the sense that he has to pay his taxes, and is an officer at the local Rotary Club down the road (though these are significant enough points). Even *as a pastor*, he has a foot in both. For he speaks for God, but he also speaks as Joe Smith, white boy from rural Indiana who spent a few years in the Navy and then as a salesman before going to seminary. He speaks to each of his congregants as to a sanctified child of God being formed in the image of Christ, but he also speaks to them as mothers, as husbands, as daughters-in-law, as jobholders, voters, cinema-goers. At every point he is navigating the intersection of their vertical dimension—their life in God—and their horizontal dimension—their life in the world. If he tries to worry about only the latter, he becomes a social gospeller with nothing to offer but narrow-minded recommendations for how to make the world a better place. If he tries to worry about only the former, he risks leaving his flock with little concrete guidance in the trials of life.

Clearly, he must do both, and attempting to draw some artificial line between "spiritual" and "civil" areas of life will not help the problem much. But he must remember that while these two are never separate, they are always *distinct*. The minister may and indeed must make prudential application of Scripture to the real-world challenges of his flock, but he must make sure that both he and they know that there is probably a fair bit of Joe Smith's midwestern biases coloring that judgment, and they themselves must, like the Bereans, search the Scriptures to see whether these things be true (Acts 17:11). In churches that have become echo-chambers (as many of ours have), few of his congregants may even think to question the equation of the pastor's opinions with

Scripture. But the error is destructive nonetheless and pastors must cultivate the practice of reading widely enough, particularly in history, to recognize where their opinions are, well, just their opinions.

But what about when the minister is faithfully proclaiming the Word, and some of the flock aren't listening? Indeed, what if some of the flock do not appear to in fact be members of the flock, but goats or even wolves who have lain hidden under a veil of hypocrisy (Matt. 25:31–45; Matt. 7:15; Acts 20:29–20)? This is where the pastor's responsibility of church discipline comes in, that thorny issue that had muddled the two-kingdoms distinction right back in the sixteenth century and which would continue to do so throughout the history of Protestantism. It is not hard to see why this issue has proved so challenging, and so easy to get wrong. In church discipline, a minister (and, depending on the tradition, his elders) attempt to make a definitive statement about the hidden, inward spiritual state of a church member; they seek to make a judgment about the spiritual kingdom, the realm in which judgment remains hidden until the eschaton. Clearly, they must seek to make this judgment on the basis of what the member has done in the outward, civil kingdom—how he has treated his wife or kids or workers.

But what is the effect of the judgment that they pronounce? To be sure, the Bible has some pretty remarkable statements about the authority of the keys (Matt. 16:19; 18:18–20; Jn. 20:23), and although we need not assume that this apostolic authority necessarily carries over to every clergymen, most Christians have drawn this conclusion. Taken at face value, passages such as Matthew 18:18 might seem to imply that when the minister excludes someone from the visible body of saints by excommunication, he severs that person from the mystical body of Christ and from salvation. Roman Catholicism certainly did understand the power of the keys in this way, but Protestants always emphasized that the keys were nothing more than the proclamation of the gospel. By proclaiming the grace of God to unworthy sinners, the minister loosed them from their bondage, and by proclaiming God's curse on the unrepentant, the minister retained them in their bondage.[2] Of course, ultimately it was the hidden work of the Spirit and the response of faith, not the mere words of the minister, that were determinative. Thus, although tasked by God with pronouncing a judgment of condemnation on unrepentant sinners, the minister's authority is only according to truth; if he errs, his sentence of condemnation or excommunication is of no effect in the spiritual kingdom. Still, church discipline, as an outward act of removing someone from the visible assembly altogether, or at least from full participation in it, does take some kind of effect regardless of the accuracy of the judgment regarding someone's inward state, and indeed often discipline is primarily for the sake of this outward effect. By removing an unruly member from the assembly of the saints, the officers of the church protect the rest of the flock against harm, and by depriving the sinner of the real benefits of membership in the visible assembly, they

---

[2] See for instance the Second Helvetic Confession, ch. XIV: "Judging simply according to the Word of the Lord, we say that all properly called ministers possess and exercise the keys or the use of them when they proclaim the Gospel; that is, when they teach, exhort, comfort, rebuke, and keep in discipline the people committed to their trust." The text can be accessed at the Christian Classics Ethereal Library, https://www.ccel.org/creeds/helvetic.htm.

may help bring him to repentance. Viewed from this standpoint, church discipline is a civil kingdom proceeding that relies on a certain kind of temporal authority (such as a civic association might have for enforcing membership vows). Both dimensions of church discipline are real and important, but it is crucial to keep in mind the distinction between the two, and the limitations of each, lest we fall into a sub-Protestant conception, in which policing the visible boundaries of the church is seen as policing the entrance to the gate of heaven.[3]

TWO KINGDOMS ECUMENISM

This temptation to confuse the visible boundaries of the church with its hidden reality often manifests itself in a subtler form: overzealous ecumenism. This is not to say that we should not be zealous for ecumenism; in John 17, Jesus prays:

> I do not ask for these only, but also for those who will believe in me through their word, that they may all be one, just as you, Father, are in me, and I in you, that they also may be in us, so that the world may believe that you have sent me. The glory that you have given me I have given to them, that they may be one even as we are one, I in them and you in me, that they may become perfectly one, so

---

[3] Jonathan Leeman's important recent book *Political Church: The Local Assembly as Embassy of Christ's Rule* (Downer's Grove, IL: IVP Academic, 2016) is an example of a treatment of this issue that fails to always avoid this ambiguity. See the fruitful interaction between Leeman and Joseph Minich at Mere Orthodoxy: https://mereorthodoxy.com/minich-leeman-joint-statement-ecclesiology/.

TWO KINGDOMS IN THE CHURCH

> that the world may know that you sent me
> and loved them even as you loved me" (Jn
> 17:20-23).[4]

This oft-quoted passage tells us at least two things about God's desire for the church. First, the unity of the church is a result of our indwelling in Christ, and is a participation in the unity of God Himself. Second, the unity of the church should be publicly displayed for the world to see; it is a way in which we witness to who Christ is. Unity is thus both hidden and manifest; it is both a given reality and a goal to be striven for.[5] Church unity, in other words, exists within the duality of the two kingdoms, and any successful ecumenism must keep both these poles in mind. If we overemphasize the given but hidden fact of the church's already-possessed unity in Christ, in the spiritual kingdom, we will feel little imperative to make it visible in the world, and the church's divided members and the watching world will suffer accordingly. On the contrary, it we overemphasize the visible manifestation and think that it is our task to *make* the church one, we will make an idol out of our ecumenical activities, and burn ourselves out in the fruitless struggle to try to achieve what Christ has already achieved and will one day Himself bring to consummation.

As James Jordan says in *The Sociology of the Church*,

> It is a fact that the church of Jesus Christ is
> unified. Jesus prayed the Father in John 17
> that we might be one, and the Father does not

---

[4] All Scripture quotations are ESV unless otherwise indicated.

[5] See also Eph. 4:1-16 for a similar is/ought dynamic in the discussion of church unity.

63

deny the petitions of the Son. Therefore, we are one. We eat of one Christ. We hearken to one Word. There is one Lord, one faith, one baptism, etc. Anyone who denies this is insane, not adjusted to reality. Thus, we cannot unite the church, and church unity is not a problem, any more than we can make America a theocracy. What we need is for people to stop pretending that the church is not united, because such a pretense is a denial of the truth. When men recognize the truth, and stop being fooled by vain appearances, then the judgment upon the church will be turned to blessing…. We cannot make the church united by negotiation. Rather, we must simply confess that the church is in truth one, and act accordingly.[6]

Just as it is mistake to think that those who are most loudly lamenting their sins are the most holy and most attuned to Christ's will, so we should beware of those who are always exhorting us to bewail the miserable and divided state of the church. In the one case, the sinner who is filled with true faith fixes his eyes not on his sin, but on the grace of Christ; and just so we should put more stock in the promises of Christ than in the depth of our divisions. Indeed, such over-pessimism, since it focuses the attention on us rather than Christ, often goes hand-in-hand with over-optimism, beginning with grim declarations of how

---

[6] James B. Jordan, *The Sociology of the Church: Essays in Reconstruction*, reprint (Eugene, OR: Wipf and Stock, 1999), 131. Thanks to Steven Wedgeworth for making me aware of this quotation.

we have grieved the Spirit and ending with rosy visions of the unity that lies before us in the decades and centuries to come.[7]

So what is the unity that we are seeking to make visible? What are we striving for? Let's consider come candidates.

Institutional unity is certainly one, and among Protestants who decry the persistence of denominations as stains of division on the body of Christ, this would seem to be particularly sought after. Of course, this is the sort of unity the Catholic Church prides itself on—a single worldwide juridical authority structure, no matter how much variation in faith and practice might be concealed under this imposing exterior. From this standpoint, it is worth asking whether the unity of the Catholic Church is really much different, or much deeper, than, say, the unity of the United States, which as we know is profoundly pluralist and polarized.

Before Vatican II, to be sure, Catholics might have claimed a second kind of unity as well, a *liturgical unity* consisting of shared practices, symbols, and rituals, preeminently the Eucharist as the sacrament of unity. This ideal of unity still prevails in the Orthodox churches, among whom it is a particular point of pride, while Catholic liturgical practice has fragmented enormously in recent decades. Many Protestants in recent decades, convicted of their own anti-liturgical tendencies, have embraced not merely a return to liturgical forms, but also

---

[7] One can see an example of both this over-optimism and over-pessimism at times in Peter Leithart's otherwise very valuable recent book *The End of Protestantism: Pursuing Unity in a Fragmented Church* (Grand Rapids: Brazos, 2016).

at times the ideal of liturgical unity as a way of knitting the body of Christ together.

A third kind of unity might be the *unity of faith*—not in the sense of the act of faith, which is indeed the one thing that unites us all to the body of Christ, but in the sense of the detailed content of faith, that is, a shared creed or pattern of belief. For many Protestants, this is the only kind of unity that matters, and indeed, until the twentieth century, Christians of nearly every stripe would have considered this essential. But opinions have always differed as to how far such unity must extend—must the true church be unified within the Westminster Confession? The Augsburg Confession? The Nicene Creed?

Finally, there is a *unity of spirit*—do Christians think of themselves as one? Act toward one another as if they are one? Do we treat one another with the love of Christ, and see ourselves as sharing a common cause and destiny? Do we work together in common mission and witness when possible, or distance ourselves from one another?

The ecumenical movement, whether in its mainline or evangelical forms, has often oscillated between these four goals, unsure which to prioritize. While each may reinforce the others, they may also be sharply at odds. For instance, the fourth, unity of spirit, often prevails more *across* institutions than *within* them, given the frequent bitterness of denominational politics. And yet is such unity enough? Mustn't it be given some concrete form?

From a Protestant two-kingdoms standpoint, we must again remember that it *is* not the church's task to make itself united, but simply to witness to its union. The church is one in Christ, the cornerstone on whom the whole building is built, the vine from which all the branches give life, the bridegroom who has bound himself to each of us (Eph. 2:20–22; Jn. 15:1–7; Eph. 5:25–32). Nothing we do can actually destroy this unity. But we can fail to manifest it as we are commanded to. "Signs must resemble the things they signify," as Richard Hooker said about the church's worship, and the same must be said of the visible church as a whole, which serves as a sign of Christ's body in the world. In pursuing the unity of the church, we aim to make the church appear, as much as possible within the limitations of its temporal form, as an image of the eschatological city.

Put another way, the Protestant ought to recognize that the task of ecumenism is always a matter of the church's sanctification, not its justification. Our divisions, however great, never threaten the *being* of the church, or our standing in Christ, but they do certainly threaten our *well-being*. Christ's spiritual rule remains intact however fragmented its earthly manifestation. Of course, this is no excuse for complacency, any more than justification by faith should entail antinomianism. On the contrary, it is an urgent summons for the church to display the unity it has in Christ, both for our own spiritual health, as we learn to love, and learn to learn from, one another, and for the integrity of our mission to the watching world. With this in mind, let us revisit our four forms of unity. Each of these, it should be noted, pertain to the outward form of the church—even the latter two, since we are concerned about unity in the faith publicly confessed, and unity of spirit manifested in love.

From a Protestant two-kingdoms standpoint, institutional unity is suspect as a goal of our ecumenical strivings.

After all, such unity is in no sense a feature of the church as the hidden body of Christ or even of the eschatological New Jerusalem, where there will be no hierarchy, laws, or disciplinary structures. The institutional form of the church is part of its outward and temporal garb, and the juridical authority needed to police the boundaries of any institution is seated firmly in the temporal kingdom of law. In this realm, local variation and regional administration are the norm, and we should be no quicker to embrace one-world church government than one-world civil government. Where many institutions jostle for position in the same geographical space, however, as typifies our modern condition, this may pose a problem, and to the extent that institutional disunity is undermining the other forms of unity, then it may be something we should seek to overcome. For instance, if two denominations who follow the same confession are jealously squabbling and competing for members, then perhaps we should campaign for a merger. But conversely, if a Lutheran and a Reformed denomination were cheerfully working alongside one another while acknowledging their differences, it is not clear why we should worry about the institutional separation *as such*. It all depends on how well *unity of faith* and *unity of spirit* govern these relations.

Liturgical unity would seem to fall under the same heading, though here the imperative for "signs to resemble the things they are signified" suggests some imperative toward unity. After all, our picture of the New Jerusalem in Revelation is a scene of worship (Rev. 4; 21:1–22:5), and our liturgies today ought to serve as dim reflections—adapted for our current condition—of the eschatological worship we will one day enjoy together. To this extent, I think we can say that there are *some* worship practices that fall outside the pale, and we must unite in excluding those (1 Cor. 14:26-40). Conversely, there are obviously certain core features of Christian worship and practice which we are bound in obedience to our Lord to maintain—the two sacraments, prayer, songs of praise, and the reading and preaching of the Word, at the very least. But Scripture provides nothing approaching a detailed blueprint for these, so the forms they take are largely prudential, and have varied enormously through time and space. Certainly it might strengthen the church's life together and its mission to cultivate more common practice on many disputed points (i.e., the charismatic gifts and the frequency of the Eucharist), but we must not mistake these forms as the ground or even the primary signs of the church's unity.

Unity of faith looms much larger. If ecumenism is a matter of the church's sanctification, and if we are justified by faith, then, it would seem, the faith of the church must be foundational, preceding the ecumenical task as a *sine qua non*. And yet, the "one faith" that does ground the church's unity must not be complexified beyond the faith that justifies, which we all know can be very lacking in doctrinal sophistication, and yet still pleasing to the Lord. In going beyond this basic confession of Christian faith, and hammering out more extensive areas of shared doctrine, we certainly aid the sanctification of the church, but must not confuse this with the definition of its essence. With the sanctification of the church, rather than its definition, in mind, we can approach questions of confessional unity more pragmatically. An individual church will require more unity of faith for its Sunday school teachers than its members, and more for its elders and deacons than for its Sunday school teachers. Two denominations trying to decide whether or not to join in a campaign to fight sex trafficking shouldn't need to agree on much beyond the basics; if they're joining in an evangelistic mission work, they will probably want to establish somewhat fuller unity of faith; and if they're creating a Sunday school curriculum, considerably more. In short, the unity of faith that we must seek depends on the particular question at hand. This is not to deny, of course, that our overarching goal should be for all Christians to be of one mind in all matters pertaining to the truth. This, however, is not the sort of thing that can be rushed or engineered, nor is it a goal we should expect to achieve this side of the eschaton. In the meantime, we must work to carefully distinguish between essentials and non-essentials, anchor our agreement on essentials, and patiently work our way outward through secondary and tertiary matters, united in charity even when divided in mind.

This leads, of course, to the final and most important type of unity, unity of spirit. Indeed, it is striking that when the Scriptures do call us to be of one mind, they seem to be concerned more with mutual love than with doctrinal uniformity:

> complete my joy by being of the same mind, having the same love, being in full accord and of one mind. Do nothing from selfish ambition or conceit, but in humility count others more significant than yourselves. Let each of you look not only to his own interests, but also to the interests of others. Have this mind

among yourselves, which is yours in Christ Jesus. (Phil. 2:2-5)

Perhaps none of the four kinds of unity highlights the distance between the church's justification and its sanctification so much as this fourth, the love that binds believers together. Nothing is so important for us to cultivate, and yet nothing so often, or so thoroughly, eludes us. In lamenting the pettiness and hatred that divides us, we must never be driven to the point of despair, since Christ promises to hold us together despite our attempts to pull apart. Neither should we fall prey to the postmodern feel-good idea of tolerance, and think that charity precludes judgment and discrimination. Christians are called to stand fast against sin and error, doing so with all charity and forbearance, but without wavering. Those who call on us to embrace in visible unity those who by word and deed spurn the cross of Christ are making an idol of visible unity, a classic two-kingdoms confusion. On the other hand, we should remember that since Christian unity can be manifested in the civil and cultural sphere just as much as in the institutional church, both falling within the temporal kingdom, we should not pooh-pooh such displays of unity as irrelevant or insignificant. When Presbyterians and Baptists and Methodists unite in picketing abortion clinics or running soup kitchens, and do so consciously as brothers and sisters in Christ, we should not think that this unity somehow "doesn't count" just because they remain distinct denominations.

Protestant ecumenism in light of the two kingdoms, then, learns to value all the outward tokens of the church's unity in their proper place, but insists on not making a fetish or an idol out of any of them.

VI:

TWO KINGDOMS IN THE STATE

WHEN THE subject of the "two kingdoms" comes up, the first thing to most people's mind is the question of politics—God vs. Caesar, church vs. state, the challenges of Christian citizenship. This is in part due to the political language of "kingdoms," in part due to the fact that the Reformers themselves often used the language of the "civil kingdom" or "political kingdom" in contrast to the "spiritual kingdom," for in their era, unlike ours, pretty much any area of life beyond the inner realm of conscience was potentially subject to the authority of the civil magistrate. For us, though, with a more circumscribed conception of the state's responsibilities, this language can be misleading, and I have thus sought to emphasize thus far the full scope of what we might better call simply the "temporal kingdom," and waited until now to broach the subject of politics.

However, the political question is clearly central to the two-kingdoms doctrine, almost as much today as it was in the Reformation era. Here the doctrine seeks to hold together the eschatological tension between Christ's insistence that "my kingdom is not of this world" (Jn. 18:36) with the triumphant declaration of Revelation that "the kingdoms of this world have become the kingdoms of our Lord and of His Christ" (Rev. 11:15, NKJV). On the one hand, there is clearly something about Christ's reign that is radically inward and hidden, that works by the transforming power of the Spirit rather than through the coercive power of the sword or the observable chains of earthly cause and effect. On the other hand, we have his promise that his reign shall not remain hidden, but at the last day shall be fully public, acknowledged by rulers and principalities.

But what about in the meantime? Does the whole political and social order lie outside of the Christian message, as some would have it? And if so, is this because the Christian message is one of radical interiority, an antinomian proclamation of grace that never becomes incarnate, as libertines would have it? Or is it because the Christian message is one of a new law and a new social order unto itself, the church as alternative community, as Anabaptists old and new would have it? Or is the political and social order subsumed into the church's proclamation, such that the gospel is not rightly preached until it has taken on flesh and bones in a renewed set of laws and institutions, and in which we can point to these renewed laws and institutions and say "here is the kingdom in our midst. Christ's reign on earth has begun." Theocrats of every age have taught such a doctrine, and it persists in a subtler form among liberal social gospellers and conservative Kuyperian worldview warriors. Classical two-kingdoms thinking eschews all these alternatives.

In outlining a two-kingdoms approach to politics, I would like to offer and briefly defend five theses:

> 1) Christ is reigning through worldly rulers and institutions to preserve his good world.
>
> 2) Christ's temporal reign is indirect and mediated in a way his spiritual reign is not.
>
> 3) Christ's temporal reign serves to guard the goodness of the created order.
>
> 4) Christ's temporal reign cannot be fully separated from his redeeming work.
>
> 5) In the political realm, we are called to witness in a distinctively Christian (but always provisional) mode to Christ's temporal reign.

Let us take each of these in turn.

1. Christ is reigning through worldly rulers and institutions to preserve his good world.

Classical two-kingdoms thinking insists that even while asserting the centrality of Christ's saving work in the church and the hearts of the faithful, we must not abandon the rest of the world to the devil, or to some spiritual no-man's land. Jesus is Caesar's Lord, and obeying Caesar can be a way of obeying Christ. Classical two-kingdoms thinking is thus a rebuke to various forms of neo-Anabaptism today that would call Christians to turn away from politics and just focus on "being the church." Indeed, it is worth noting that some contemporary Christians in America, burnt-out on Religious Right politics or frustrated by the hypocrisy of the Republican Party, have gone a good deal further than historic Anabaptism in their rejection of civil authority. The Anabaptist Schleitheim Confession of 1527, after all, declared that,

> The sword is ordained of God outside the perfection of Christ. It punishes and puts to death the wicked, and guards and protects the good. In the Law the sword was ordained for the punishment of the wicked and for their death, and the same [sword] is [now] ordained to be used by the worldly magistrates. In the perfection of Christ, however, only the ban is used for a warning and for the excommunication of the one who has sinned, without putting the flesh to death—simply the warning and the command to sin no more.[1]

Christians, following the "perfection of Christ," must not only practice a different kind of non-carnal discipline in their own communities, but must decline to serve as magistrates. Still, the confession affirms that the magistrate and his coercion have been "ordained of God" for a good and necessary purpose.

You can argue that it is odd and incoherent to maintain that there could be a good, God-given office which is only supposed to be held by God-haters, but such a position at least recognizes the crucial role of civil authority in preserving the creation order and providing a

---

[1] Michael Sattler, *The Brotherly Agreement of a Number of Children of God Concerning Seven Articles*, trans. J.C. Wenger, http://www.anabaptists.org/history/the-schleitheim-confession.html.

context in which the church can flourish. Many Christians today are not so sure, with contemporary forms of pacifism often arguing categorically against the use of physical coercion, insisting that civil magistrates too are bound to govern in a way that does not involve the use of the sword, and calling for a "eucharistic anarchism."[2] It is unclear what this might mean in practice—it would seem to reduce the state to nothing more than a Public Information Bureau, issuing admonitions about what seems like the best course of action for society and which behaviors should on balance be avoided. Most of those engaging in such rhetoric, however, have not been terribly concerned to flesh out their concrete proposals, since their purpose has been to downplay the state as a site of God's government and action, and emphasize the church community alone as the agent of world-renewal.

Of course, it is true in a properly-qualified sense, as we have seen, to speak of the church community as an agent of world-renewal, but what world? If there are no legitimate structures and institutions for preserving the social order of this world, then there is nothing out there to be renewed; there is only the church.

---

[2] The term is used by William T. Cavanaugh in his essay "The City: Beyond Secular Parodies," in *Radical Orthodoxy*, ed. John Milbank, Catherine Pickstock, and Graham Ward (Abingdon: Routledge, 1999), 194–98, though he has since stated he regrets using the term (personal conversation, 2010). Of course, such neo-Anabaptists have been anything but clear in how far they want their pacifism to extend (Stanley Hauerwas being a prominent example of an ethicist who seems at times to treat pacifism as a distinctive ethic of the church and at other times as an ethic for the world). See Andrew Fulford, *Jesus and Pacifism* (Moscow, ID: The Davenant Press, 2016), 15–18 for a helpful attempt to disentangle different pacifist rationales.

Leaving aside the stronger forms of neo-Anabaptism, though, how does classical two-kingdoms theology challenge classical Anabaptism, and, for that matter, neo-two-kingdoms theology? For in fact, I would argue, some modern forms of Reformed two-kingdoms theology share key assumptions with the Schleitheim Confession. Key to that confession is the distinction between the "ordinance of God" and the "perfection of Christ." There are, we are told, two parallel tracks of this-worldly social order and morality: one that corresponds to creation order and one that corresponds to the new creation; one which is outside of Christ's redemptive work and one that is within it.[3]

This way of thinking, in my view, not only creates some curious conundrums for ethics, but introduces serious problems into fundamental areas of theology. Either the unity of the Trinity is compromised, by inappropriately setting the activity of God the Father and the activity of God the Son against one another, or the unity of Christ's person is compromised, by inappropriately setting Christ's divine nature as the eternal *logos* against his incarnate form as Christ the Redeemer. In fact, it is striking that certain early modern Reformed thinkers in the Puritan strand of two-kingdoms thinking did precisely this, insisting that Christ rules the world as eternal God, but the church as incarnate man. This is so much so that, as David

---

[3] See for instance David VanDrunen, "Calvin, Kuyper, and 'Christian Culture'," in *Always Reformed: Essays in Honor of W. Robert Godfrey*, ed. R. Scott Clark and Joel E. Kim (Escondido, CA: Westminster Seminary California, 2010), 148–49; Darryl G. Hart, "With Friends Like These," Oldlife.org, July 20, 2015, https://oldlife.org/2015/07/20/with-friends-like-these/. VanDrunen is considerably more nuanced in his recent *Divine Covenants and Moral Order: A Biblical Theology of Natural* (Grand Rapids: Eerdmans, 2015), but I still have some reservations about the way he formulates his "eschatological ethic" in ch. 9.

VanDrunen puts it, we cannot speak of Christ as "Christ" in his world-governing capacity, since this is a redemptive title.[4] Against this, however, Richard Hooker, following 1 Cor. 15:24–28, says, "The works of supreme Dominion which have been since the first beginning wrought by the power of the Son of God are now most truly and properly the works of the Son of man. The *word* made *flesh* doth sit forever and reign as Sovereign *Lord* over all."[5]

This might seem like an abstract theological debate, but it has concrete ramifications for how we understand politics and Christian citizenship, as we shall see when we come to the fourth point below.

2. Christ's temporal reign is indirect and mediated in a way his spiritual reign is not.

Just as it is important to insist that political authority bears the authority of God in Christ, it is equally important to insist that it does so in a highly indirect way and with many limitations. The most basic distinction here is to say that although the *office* of political authority is ratified by God, this does not mean that any particular exercise of that office necessarily is. The particular human beings who hold political office still make their particular decisions as human beings, with all the fallibility belonging to mere mortals, and their commands only bind us to the extent that those commands approximate the God-given ends of political authority. Of course, this does not mean that their commands are only as valid as any old Tom, Dick, or

---

[4] *Natural Law and the Two Kingdoms*, 180–81, 313–14.

[5] Hooker, *Lawes*, VII.4.6, http://oll.libertyfund.org/titles/hooker-the-works-of-richard-hooker-vol-3.

Harry who says, "The most just thing for everyone to do would clearly be X." There is no room to enter into a complete theory of political authority here, but part of what it means for civil authority to be divinely authorized is that the lawgiver's discretionary authority must overrule all other merely discretionary authority; when the legislature says, "It would be a good idea if everyone did this," obedience becomes more than just a good idea (unless direct injustice has been decreed).

Of course, we today in the West probably do not need to be told that political authorities are fallen and fallible, and do not speak with the voice of Christ himself. But this does not mean we are immune to subtler forms of a confusion of the two kingdoms here. Christians are often tempted to exalt their own prudential judgments for the best kind of legislation into biblical mandates and to extol leaders who enact these judgments as the only valid choice for Christian voters. Sometimes entire institutions or nations have been able to capture the imagination of Christians longing to see the reign of God, and have deceived us into thinking that these governments enjoyed a special divine blessing and calling and were the unique agents of the divine will, a deception that usually ends in tragedy and deeply harms the Christian witness. For Christians in America, with our sense of divine mission from the beginning and our tendency toward millenarian-ism, this has been a recurrent temptation.

Even when political authorities or earthly institutions are indeed doing the will of God, they remain fragile and fallible, not something that we can never grasp hold of and say, "here indeed is the Kingdom."

3. Christ's temporal reign serves to guard the goodness of the created order.

Although we noted above that Christ's reign over creation should not be separated from his role as redeemer (and we will say more about this in a moment), still it is true that the main objective of Christ's temporal reign is to sustain, protect, and nourish the goodness of creation order, and this is particularly the task of civil authority. When we speak of "creation order," it is important to lay equal stress on both words. This world bears the stamp of and points to its creator, but it also has an intrinsic ordered structure of its own, as does every creature within it. It is this order which God looks at in Genesis 1 and pronounces "good." Corrupted though the world may be by the fall, most of this order remains quite intact and recognizable. Trees still grow upward, water still flows downward, plants still yield seed according to their kind, the creeping things still creep on the earth, and human beings still exercise dominion over all of this. More relevantly for purposes of political rule, human nature too remains broadly intact. We are still male and female, marry and bear children, tend the earth, make tools and make music; it is still not good for us to be alone and so we form communities and seek to order our lives together for mutual flourishing. Of course, here above all the Fall has affected the conditions under which we seek such flourishing; we must now contend with scarcity and jealousy, rivalries and ambition, stubbornness, pride, and malice.

Political authority is rendered indispensable under these conditions as God's ordained means of restraining and disciplining our disordered desires, so that some semblance of the original good order of humanity might be maintained, and that, in the words of one church Father, "men may not eat each other up like fishes."[6] But the fact that political authority must now use coercion does not mean that political rule is amoral or free-floating, making things up according to the demands of *realpolitik*. No, it is still bound to the moral order of the world as God created it, and must reflect that as much as possible. Nor is it the case that government exists simply as a kind of electric fence to restrain incursions against creation order, as if that order otherwise took care of itself. Some political theologies that seek to base civil authority solely on the Noahic Covenant, with its minimal commands, or on libertarian preconceptions, commit this error.[7]

Because civil government's task is rooted in the maintenance of creation order, it follows that however valuable Scripture may be for informing this task, it is not *necessary*. The general norm of political rule is natural revelation and natural law,[8] not Scripture, although Scripture, as a remedy to our fallenness, restates many of the principles of natural law, along with instructive examples of good and bad government. Accordingly, Christians do not have anything like a monopoly on good

---

[6] Irenaeus of Lyons, *Against Heresies*, Book 5, in O'Donovan and O'Donovan, *From Irenaeus to Grotius*, 17.

[7] David VanDrunen, who has tended this way in some of his work, tries to nuance in his recent *Divine Covenants and Moral Order*, ch. 2, arguing that the Noahic Covenant "focuses upon a bare minimalist ethic concerning intrahuman affairs, designed to preserve the existence of human society," while also acknowledging that the maintenance of a broader moral order will be needed to maintain society (123). He never really clearly integrates these "thin" and "thick" conceptions of moral and social order, however.

[8] For more on natural law, see our forthcoming Davenant Guide on the subject by Andrew Fulford later this year.

government, and indeed, Christian naïveté, idealism, or otherworldliness sometimes makes us downright terrible at the task of governing. But this does not mean that political government can really be religiously neutral. After all, although we have stressed the "order" part of the phrase "creation order," the "creation" part is just as crucial. The order of this world only makes sense in the end as an order bestowed by and pointing toward a Creator, and earthly rulers who forget this are liable to soon forget the order as well. Even the minimalist Noahic Covenant begins with a sacrifice to God in grateful acknowledgment to him of his sustenance of the world (Genesis 8:20–21). Even in the seemingly self-sufficient modern liberal West, our political structures cannot long do without such grateful acknowledgment of their Lord before they try to set themselves up as lords in His place.

4. Christ's temporal reign cannot be fully separated from his redeeming work.

But is this all that Christianity has to say to politics—that is must safeguard the order which God has built into the world and in some way acknowledge its Creator? Many two-kingdoms thinkers seem to think so, emphasizing the contrast of "creation" and "redemption" as the division between the two kingdoms, and warning that redemption has nothing to do with the temporal kingdom or the task of politics. However, this seems to forget that "redeem" is a transitive verb, and Scripture is quite clear that the object of this redemption is not merely the souls of believers, but the whole created order (Rom. 8:19–22). To be sure, the application of redemption begins in the souls of believers, but it works its way outward (though never close to fully until the consummation). The world is broken, and is being healed. Political rulers ought not seek to pre-empt the shape of the new creation, but neither must they rest content with a fully broken world; inasmuch as Scripture reveals and the gospel enables a world ordered as it was originally meant to be, politics may be guided by this ideal and nourished by this Christian virtue.

Or, to put it another way, because Christ reigns over the kingdoms of this world *as the one who is their redeemer*, sustaining the creation order precisely so that his redemptive work can be brought to completion within it, this shapes the mission of earthly rulers. Properly speaking, the rulers of the kingdoms of this world, mediating as they do the authority of Christ, are likewise responsible for sustaining the creation order *for the sake of* its redemption. Their task is not to try and achieve this redemption, but neither should they be wholly indifferent to it. Their office is only coherent if it has a purpose or end—sustaining the creation order—and this end is only coherent if it is itself directed toward a final end—the consummation of this order. Now this does not mean that civil authority cannot function at all, or even function often quite well, without explicit awareness of this end. Just as a caretaker charged to maintain a great country estate could in principle do his job quite well without knowing the fact that the king himself purposed to move there soon and make it his residence, so magistrates can recognize that order is better than disorder, and work to maintain order accordingly, without knowing the purpose of that order. Still, at some point someone is liable to say, "What's the point of all this?" and if they do not have the true answer provided by the Christian gospel, are liable to either let things go to ruin, or treat political order as an arbitrary and self-serving assertion of power. And just as the caretaker will do some things differently if he knows the house is intended to be the residence of the king, so civil authorities will do their task somewhat differently (including privileging and protecting the church in contextually-appropriate ways) if they know that they are stewards of the coming king.

5. In the political realm, we are called to witness in a distinctively Christian (but always provisional) mode to Christ's temporal reign.

So what does all this mean for us, for ordinary Christian citizens in our communities and voting booths, or for Christians serving at all levels of government, as police-men, tax collectors, judges, or senators? Most of what I have said thus far in this chapter has fallen under the heading of a Christian theory of civil government, not a blueprint for Christian practice. This is unavoidable in a book like this, which is meant to be a slender guide, and hence must focus on principles more than practical prescriptions. It is also intentional given one of the key theses of this book, which is that the temporal kingdom is characterized by prudence, by a Spirit-filled wisdom that creatively responds to the challenges posed by each new circumstance.

Still, even if we must remain at the level of principles, we can distill from what we have said already four more *practical* principles for two-kingdoms politics at the level of the individual citizen, loosely corresponding to the four points above. The first is we cannot be quietists; love of neighbor in our context demands that Christians be willing to take action in the public square, whether as leaders or as engaged citizens holding our leaders to account and challenging them to love justice and serve their people.

The second is that when we do take this action, we must do so *as Christians*, as redeemed children of God, who by virtue of this redemption recognize the limited claims that civil authority can make on us. We are not under law, but under grace, and though this does not exclude an ongoing role for human law, this law should not terrify us or seem burdensome. If the law is just, we should cheerfully embrace it as the means by which we love our neighbor. If the law is unjust, we should challenge it for the sake of our Lord and our neighbor without fearing the consequences. We can and sometimes must say to our authorities, "You would have no authority over me at all unless it had been given to you from above," (Jn. 19:11) reminding them whose ministers they are.

Third, just because we enter the public square *as Christians*, this does not mean our only standard is Scripture. We should not expect ready-made solutions from Scripture to the challenges of the 21st century, nor should we forget that most political prudence comes from nature, not grace. We can and usually should appeal to reason, to history, to constitutions, to evidence showing the bad results of certain policies, seeking to persuade our opponents rather than beat them over the head with the Bible. Note that this would be true *even in a Christian society*, as Richard Hooker argues, for Scripture provides relatively little guidance on the details of public policy. But it is all the more the case in a pluralistic society where we cannot count on others to share our convictions. But neither should we pretend to a total neutrality or ignore the value of our faith in forming and filling out our political reflections, and we should be prepared to admit, when pressed, that yes, our belief in Scripture compels us to take a certain position—say, on the sanctity of unborn life—even if, we contend, that is a truth that should be evident in nature itself.

Fourth, our engagement with politics should be measured and realistic, recognizing the provisionality of the political order. Perhaps the greatest error of evangelicals in the past generation has been the temptation to think that more could be achieved through politics than was realistic, and sometimes that more *must* be achieved through politics than was appropriate. It goes without saying that we should not expect radical transformation of the temporal order into the new Jerusalem; it can only ever hint at and witness to Christ's reign, not incarnate it. We all admit this, no doubt, but we often seem to expect politics to change hearts, which is of course Christ's prerogative alone, and without changed hearts, many otherwise good policies may prove futile. This conclusion need not entail a libertarian minimalism about the kinds of things that government can address, but it should entail a sober realism about how effective those efforts will prove on their own.

But we should note that this point itself is perhaps the most important, and potentially revolutionary, Christian contribution to politics. For the natural temptation of earthly politics is always to claim for itself an ultimacy it cannot sustain, or make redemptive promises it cannot deliver. Once religious faith ebbs in a people, political messianism and its evil twin, political apocalypticism, begin to flourish. Precisely by pointing to an excess that always lies beyond politics, two-kingdoms thinking promises to reshape political life even at its most apolitical.

VII:
TWO KINGDOMS IN THE MARKET

CHRIST AND MAMMON

IF POLITICS is the most obvious domain to consider what it means for Christians to live in the temporal kingdom, perhaps the most important for our day-to-day discipleship is economics, or more generally, money matters. In few areas, indeed, are distorted versions of the two kingdoms distinction more common or more damaging. The contrast between the free grace of the gospel extolled in our pulpits, forgiving the debts of every sin, and the hard-nosed financial savvy extolled almost everywhere else, seizing every opportunity for lawful profit, is so sharp that we prefer to compartmentalize if at all possible. Even preachers who don't hesitate to tackle other cultural and political topics often tend to tactfully steer clear of financial subjects, except perhaps on one or two Sundays a year, in which they try to soften up their congregants in anticipation of annual giving pledges.

And yet cutting across any of our attempts to self-consolingly divvy up the terrain between the two kingdoms comes our Lord's disconcerting words, "No one can serve two masters, for either he will hate the one and love the other, or he will be devoted to the one and despise the other. You cannot serve God and money" (Mt. 6:24). Whatever we are to say about the two kingdoms, they are *Christ's* two kingdoms after all, over both of which he reigns as sole King, and in both of which he demands our undivided love and service. While Mammon may have set up outposts in every corner of the earthly kingdom, requiring us to navigate this landscape with great care and prudence, we must not concede its mastery at any point. The question then becomes how we can use wealth without yielding it a love and service it does not deserve. We must also beware the temptation of thinking that we can resolve the tension by means of some two-track morality like the medieval distinction between *counsels* and *commandments*. In this scheme, commands such as "Sell all that you have and give to the poor," (Mk. 10:21) and the example of the Jerusalem church in Acts, became the code of morality for those who wished to be particularly holy, while everyone else was allowed to operate on a more minimalist standard. We often do this today by convenient compartmentalizations of justice and charity, in which the first means simply obeying the law and respecting private property, and the latter means helping out the poor or contributing to a ministry if you feel spontaneously moved to do so and want to be extra godly.

Such schemes all reflect a fundamental confusion, however. Christian morality is not some arbitrary extra to gain brownie points with God. Rather, it is a summons to leave the road that leads to destruction and take the road that leads to life. Idolatry is objectively destructive, and those whose financial lives are characterized by idolatry will shipwreck their financial lives, not just their spiritual lives. This does not mean that we cannot distinguish between things that are basic universal commands and obligations that vary by circumstance, but the difference flows not from whether you want to choose the "Easy" or "Hard" difficulty setting for the Christian life, but simply from the variation in our concrete callings and circumstances. The command to "care for the poor" may take on a different form for each particular Christian, given their means, opportunities, temptations, and other commitments, but the basic obligation applies to all. Any version of two-kingdoms theology that allows Christians to apply one moral standard in the church and a different one to the rest of life is missing the point. As we have seen throughout this book, since the basic distinction between the two kingdoms is internal and external, *both* come into play at every point of the Christian life, but in different ways. Here, as elsewhere, the distinction stands as a rebuke to legalism but also does not authorize for a moment antinomianism. But the deep and subtle temptations that Mammon poses make this line a particularly difficult one to walk when it comes to our financial lives.

As a part-time investment advisor and a part-time writer and teacher on Christian ethics, I have been keenly aware of the tension between Mammon's claims and God's for many years. And it is not a tension easily dispelled by prophetic rants against upper-class greed or middle-class complacency. Does setting aside money for kids' college, instead of giving all your surplus away and trusting God, count as service of Mammon? What about saving for a long and comfortable retirement? What about shrewdly weighing your investment options for maximal return, rather than investing in your Christian friend's business, or spending extravagantly on Christmas gifts for friends and family? These are not easy questions.[1] In this chapter, I hope to shed just a bit of light on how we might go about answering some of them, or at least forming our consciences to become the kind of people who can answer them rightly in our own unique callings.

CONFUSING THE TWO KINGDOMS IN MONEY MATTERS

It should be clear that without any two-kingdoms distinction when it comes to our financial lives, the dangers are myriad. In the prosperity gospel, preachers conflate God's spiritual blessings on believers for their faith with worldly prosperity. In some forms of what we might call "Christo-capitalism,"[2] the dynamic force of the market becomes the engine of God's redemptive purposes in history, and the Bible is prostituted to economic ideology to encourage an almost religious faith in free-market mechanisms.[3] Alternatively, on the left side of the politico-economic spectrum, many Christians aim to apply the logic of the "divine economy" of unconditional giving

---

[1] For further reflections, see my "Dependent or Independent? Towards a Christian Way of Thinking about Saving and Wealth," *Journal of Markets and Morality* 19, no. 2 (Winter 2016): 389–99.

[2] The term comes from Elizabeth Stoker Bruenig, "Christo-Capitalism or Capitalanity? David Brat's Political Theology," *Political Theology Today*, June 19, 2014, http://www.politicaltheology.com/blog/christo-capitalism/.

[3] Examples include Jay Richards, *Money, Greed, and God: Why Capitalism is the Solution, Not the Problem* (New York: HarperCollins, 2009), and Shawn Ritenour, *Foundations of Economics: A Christian View* (Eugene, OR: Wipf and Stock Publishers, 2010).

to the earthly economic order, hoping to eradicate need and social conflict, and thus incarnate Christ's kingdom on earth, or else buy into forms of liberation theology in which poverty and righteousness, wealth and depravity are crudely equated.[4]

However, if the two-kingdoms distinction is simply conflated with the institutional distinction between church and state, other problems can arise. Anabaptism, both in its sixteenth-century form and its fashionable recent incarnations, thinks that, if the church is the spiritual kingdom, it can anticipate in its own earthly life the shape of the coming reign of Christ. Accordingly it may seek to abolish private property in favor of a community of goods, and become a "scarcity-free" economy unto itself, with frequently tragic results. Or, for many recent "R2K" advocates, the doctrine is used primarily to keep any redemptive aspirations out of the economic policies of the state, which is to serve as a minimalist guardian of order.[5] Unsurprisingly, then, this use of the paradigm has proved popular among politically conservative Reformed folks. More troublingly, it has also been used to underwrite a minimalistic approach to Christian charity: deacons distribute charity within the institutional church, but should not minister to the broader world;[6] and since for some conservatives, the state should not be involved in the

---

[4] Examples include Kathryn Tanner, *Economy of Grace* (Minneapolis: Fortress, 2005) and Douglas M. Jones, *Dismissing Jesus: How we Evade the Way of the Cross* (Eugene, OR: Cascade, 2013). The classic statement of liberation theology is Gustavo Gutierrez, *A Theology of Liberation: History, Politics, and Salvation*, trans. John Eagleson (Maryknoll, NY: Orbis, 1973).

[5] See especially Hart, *From Billy Graham to Sarah Palin.*

welfare business either, this leaves no one to care for the poor.

Both of these general approaches must be rejected. Against the first error, confusing redemptive grace with market mechanism, we must maintain a clear distinction between the already of Christ's reign, which is hidden, and the not yet, which will one day be made manifest, and between the norms of nature that govern our economic lives and the norms of grace that govern our spiritual lives (though, without rendering the latter irrelevant to the former). God does desire humanity to flourish and enjoy the bounties of creation given into our care and for our use, and so we can and should see a just and prosperous economic system as one of his blessings. But it is a benefit of common grace, a shower that falls often on the evil as well as the good. When Proverbs sometimes associates prosperity with riches (e.g., Prov. 8:18, 21; 13:22; 15:6), this is more an observation about natural cause and effect— virtuous behavior tends to lead to success—than a *quid pro quo* promise of divine reward. Although superficially pointing in the opposite direction, liberation theology makes the same basic category mistake, assuming that material poverty is a mark of God's favor, but also somewhat paradoxically, that the alleviation of this poverty *is* what Christ's redemption means, and that wherever economic justice happens, Christ's kingdom has come. All of this represents an attempt to bring the life of the world to come into the present.

On the same note, we must also beware of making Scripture speak too comprehensively or bindingly to

---

[6] See for instance VanDrunen, *Living in God's Two Kingdoms*, 158–59.

matters of economic life. Both on the Right and on the Left, one can find scores of books claiming to give an economics according to the Bible, one which always turns out to look suspiciously like one of the prevailing economic and political theories on offer in the modern marketplace of ideas. Liberation theologians always manage to find the ideas of Marx spelled out in Scripture, while conservative Reformed theologians seem to always manage to find the ideas of von Mises and Hayek. But both errors are equally absurd. For the classical two-kingdoms theorist, there is no *prima facie* reason to assume that we should find an economic theory in Scripture. If, however, we do as a matter of fact find various insights and norms for economic life (and I think we certainly do), we must remember that norms governing changeable circumstances only bind insofar as the circumstances are the same. There is certainly insight to be gained from the sabbath-year laws for contemporary debt-relief, for instance, but not a direct prescription, since the same principles might suggest different legal application in our own circumstances.

But if we must beware the danger of over-spiritualizing the world, we must equally resist the second kind of error, that of over-spiritualizing the church community over against the world. When it comes to money, we must once again recognize that the visible church itself straddles the two kingdoms. After all, churches too must make budgets, maintain bank accounts, ensure careful accountability in the use of funds, make cost-benefit analyses when confronted with a multitude of needs, etc. They are not somehow magically exempted from the ordinary conditions and constraints of earthly life, comprising a sacred bubble within which a "divine economy" can take shape (Acts 6:1–4; 1 Tim. 5:3–16). Church deacons and Christian charities have not been bestowed with the ability to make one dollar turn into two, or granted immunity toward the temptations of greed, embezzlement, and wastefulness. Nor does a building project, conference, or retreat become any less extravagant and any more deserving of the faithful Christian's funds just because it is pursued by a church. The church may be the gateway of Christ's kingdom, but it is at the same time a thoroughly mundane and fallible human institution.

This alone is an important practical insight of the two-kingdoms doctrine. It is an open secret that many churches or Christian ministries are abysmal stewards of their money, imagining that just because they are doing Christ's work, they can dispense with basic dictates of prudence. But still, by shrouding themselves in an aura of sanctity, they keep a stubborn hold over the consciences of believers, who often continue to shell out vast sums of money, with very little accountability, for Christian ministries and institutions. Many blame this problem on parachurch ministries, and to be sure, these are often particularly free from accountability and thus rife with abuse. But similar situations occur almost as frequently in denominations and local churches as well. In every church and ministry undertaking, Christians must beware that in their quest to follow in Jesus' footsteps and multiply the loaves, they do not repeat the sad saga of the man who, desiring to build a tower, did not sit down and count the cost (Lk. 14:28–30).

Likewise, although I do not want to give up any aspiration to apply a sacrificial, Christ-like logic in the economics of our Christian communities, these remain very much *simul justus et peccator*, rendering Anabaptist utopianism, well, utopian. At the same time, though, if we refuse to equate institutional church and spiritual kingdom, as I argue here, this will blur the boundaries somewhat between church ministries and social action generally. Some two-kingdoms theorists want to erect a high wall between deacons dispensing sacred charity to the saints, on the one hand, and soup kitchens, service projects in the slums, or building wells in Haiti, on the other hand. But it is difficult to find historical support for such a division. Calvin's deacons in Geneva were as much civic functionaries as church officers, and the General Hospital and *Bourse Francaise* which they oversaw were comprehensive welfare institutions.[7] There may be good prudential reasons for limiting the diaconal work of the institutional church to providing for needs very close to home, but if so, others in the body of believers need to step up and creatively extend the reach of Christian charity throughout their communities and the world.

HOW THE TWO KINGDOMS SHOULD SHAPE OUR ECONOMIC LIVES

Although I have cautioned repeatedly against an over-spiritualizing of economic life, does that mean that the Christian has nothing distinctive to contribute, that he gives his tithe on Sunday but the other six days of the

---

[7] See Lewis, "Calvinism in Geneva," 44–45, and for a full treatment of the *Bourse Francaise*, Jeannine E. Olson, *Calvin and Social Welfare: Deacons and the Bourse Francaise* (Selinsgrove, PA: Susquehanna University Press, 1988).

week simply follows the gods of self-interest and efficiency? Well, no. Here I will draw upon two points related to those I made in the previous chapter.

First, I noted that although it should not anticipate the *new creation*, the temporal kingdom is bound to the norms of the original creation, so that inasmuch as redemption heals the distortions of our fallen vision and shows us how we were meant to live as humans, it will point us back to the appropriate ways to order our earthly societies (within the limitations of our depravity). A two-kingdoms perspective should never be misunderstood as a license to be lukewarm about social and economic justice, rightly understood. We do live in a social order that has been disordered by sin and greed, and Christians should have more urgency than anyone in wanting to confront these corruptions. But since these are corruptions of old creation order, not failures to conform to new creation order (which will indeed transcend the dynamics of scarcity that govern this-worldly economics), they should be confronted on the terms of nature, rather than grace. It is interesting to see how often, when you find modern idealists calling for a transformed "divine economy," most of what they describe fits what older thinkers would have described as "natural law"—i.e., community over individual, an end to usury, equity for the poor. Christians *should* challenge the perversions of our contemporary economy, but on the basis that it is unnatural, not that it is un-cruciform.

Second, I noted that the very apolitical nature of the spiritual kingdom can have a radical effect on politics, by reminding us of its limitations, its provisionality. The same goes for our economic life. The Christian too must enter into the worldly rhythms of supply and demand, of debt and savings, of profit and loss, and navigate them with all due prudence; but the Christian does this knowing that his true treasure is in heaven, where moth and rust do not destroy (Matt. 6:19–20). Most of the perversions of our economic lives come simply from idolizing them, treating money as an end rather than a means. As Christ's spiritual reign frees us from this bondage, it enables us to walk through his temporal kingdom as pilgrims, using the goods of this world for Him and our neighbor, but not seeking our good in them. It is not as though Christ's command to the Rich Young Ruler was (as sometimes taught) a unique commandment that only applied to him. Rather, we are *all* called to live as if our goods are not our own, but our neighbor's, using all that we possess for the good of others (beginning, of course, with our families, though not ending there); it's just most of us are called to do so while still retaining a legal title to our possessions, while for some, a more radical course of action may be needed (cf. Matt. 27:57–60; Acts 4:32–37; Acts 5:1–5; Acts. 16:11–15).

If we faithfully pursue this conviction, we will refute the objection that emphasizing the "inward" character of Christ's commands minimalizes them or gives us a free pass from actually living self-sacrificially. Consider how the Reformers understood the eighth commandment. In his Small Catechism, Martin Luther writes: "You shall not steal. *What does this mean?* We should fear and love God so that we do not take our neighbor's money or possessions, or get them in any dishonest way, *but help him to improve and protect his possessions and income.*"[8] The Heidelberg Catechism

---

[8] http://catechism.cph.org/en/10-commandments.html. Latter italics mine.

sings the same tune in Q. 111: "Q. What does God require of you in this commandment? A. That I do whatever I can for my neighbor's good, that I treat others as I would like them to treat me, and that I work faithfully so that I may share with those in need."[9]

Christian life lived in the temporal kingdom, precisely because it is lived *in light* of the spiritual kingdom and on the basis of the liberating verdict of justification, is not an ethic of minimalist justice that just refrains from harming others. It is an ethic of active love that seeks the good of others (without disregarding the appropriate self-interest that maintains our ability to *continue* helping others) in every domain. If I am in a position to price my product, or pay my workers, at a level that maximizes my profit and leaves others the slimmest of margins, I must recognize this as a temptation to violate the eighth commandment. Likewise, if I can afford to bless someone by buying a product and tipping generously, well there's an opportunity to obey the eighth commandment. This is not how we Americans like to work—we're happy to give generously later, we tell ourselves, but when it's time to do business, we want to make sure we don't leave any money on the table. And often we baptize this sort of thinking with a muddled version of the two-kingdoms, telling ourselves that since business falls within the temporal kingdom, we can adopt the standards of the world and set aside the imperatives of Christ. But of course, leaving some money on the table—or some grain at the corners of the fields— is exactly how God told Israel to practice their charity.

---

[9]   https://www.crcna.org/welcome/beliefs/confessions/heidelberg-catechism.

VIII:
CONCLUSION

SOME readers may be apt to be a bit disappointed by the argument of this book, and of its second half in particular. For Christians urgently seeking guidance about whom they should vote for, or how the church should respond to war, or capitalism, or socialism, or encroachments on religious liberty, or the myriad social and political challenges that face Christians today, I have offered no concrete guidance. Nor have I even accomplished the lesser task of defining, in some timeless way, what matters belong to the state and what matters to the church, or settling how much common ground believers should seek with unbelievers in matters of culture and politics. Part of this, of course, is due to the slender size of this book; this book is no more than an invitation to modern Christians to begin an exploration of a long-neglected and oft-misunderstood doctrine. But part of this is due to the doctrine itself.

I argued in Chapter Four that, at its most basic, the two-kingdoms doctrine was a challenge to idolatry, to the constant temptation to invest secondary matters with primary significance, mundane matters with eternal implications. As such, the two-kingdoms doctrine is above all a call to recover the exercise of prudence and wisdom, freed by the Spirit to creatively re-apply Biblical principles and precedents to situations and questions where God has not always supplied us with detailed blueprints and timeless answers. The history of Christianity is one of trying to write appendices or footnotes to Scripture whenever we feel that the Bible has not adequately addressed questions that we feel need answering. The medieval church did this by elevating unwritten traditions and the interpretive authority of the papacy, in order to add myriad doctrines and practices that were now required of believers although not found in Scripture. Protestants, having defined themselves in reaction to such overreach, were still tempted to commit the same kind of error, though usually in the opposite direction—by insisting that whatever Scripture did not command, or whatever might tempt one to violate Scriptural commands, was thereby forbidden (alcohol, dancing, celebrating the church calendar, singing hymns in worship, etc.). Some versions of two-kingdoms doctrine today function the same way, serving to define long lists of things that the church cannot do and that the state cannot do, without clear Scriptural justification.

But what then can we say to the objection, which I also anticipated in Chapter Four, that our fundamental problem today is not that which the Reformers faced? Theirs was a world dominated by a ubiquitous and sometimes oppressive sense of the sacred, one where God, the Devil, or at least a saint might be lurking around every corner, and one where churchmen did not hesitate to make extraordinary claims to authority, claims which held many souls in bondage. Ours, however, is a world from which the sacred has been banished, where even most Christians don't even think about encountering the sacred outside of Sunday mornings, and where the authority of churches and pastors seems anemic next to the all-powerful voice of individual judgment. Idolatry may be a danger in every age, but the idolatry of our age is the idolatry of the individual, not of people, places, institutions, and texts. The task of theology today, then, must be to re-enchant the structures of the earthly kingdom so that they might again become conduits of God's grace and authority. So the objection runs.

There is some justice in this objection, to be sure. Our battles are not the same as Luther's, and our tactics must be different. He needed to remind people of the all-too-human element in the visible church, where as we often need to remind people of the divine element. Still, the objection is misguided, on at least two fronts. First, it misunderstands the two-kingdoms doctrine, as should hopefully be clear to anyone who has read this far. The two-kingdoms doctrine does not accept a full-scale "disenchantment" of the world, a flat, dreary, mundane temporal realm from which the sacred has been evacuated. No, as we have insisted throughout, the temporal kingdom is one in which God constantly manifests himself through "masks" (Luther's term) and "signs" (Hooker's term)—the institutions of the visible church foremost among them. The temporal life of the people of God, moreover, was for the Reformers irreducibly social and communal; never did they countenance the kind of radical individualism that has corroded all forms and concepts of authority in the modern West. Indeed, the idea that one must somehow surround an authority with a spiritual-kingdom aura before it can be taken seriously is simply evidence of how

degraded—and how far from traditional Protestantism—
our anthropology and ethics have become. It should also
be noted that the two-kingdoms doctrine is in no way tied
to a "low-church" ecclesiology, in the sense of a minimalist
liturgy and sacramentology. The example of Richard
Hooker is proof enough that a determination to carefully
distinguish signs (temporal) from things signified (spiritual)
in no way prevents one from giving a robust defense of
the importance and value of those signs.

Second, however, the objection also underestimates
the extent to which, even in our supposedly modern
disenchanted world, the search for sacred people, places,
institutions, and texts continues unabated. Indeed, the
spiritual emptiness of modern culture has intensified this
search for many people, as evidenced in phenomena as
diverse as the revival of Islamic fundamentalism, political
messianism on both right and left, identity politics that
sacralize gayness or blackness or whiteness or femininity,
the rise of cult movements and celebrity pastors, and much
else. To all such idolatries, the two-kingdoms doctrine
must remain our answer.

Indeed, the most important thing to be said in defense of the contemporary relevance of the two-kingdoms
doctrine is that it is *true*, and truth must always be
proclaimed. As we have seen in this book, the two-
kingdoms doctrine, rightly understood, is inseparably
wrapped up with what it means to be a Protestant, and to
proclaim the truth of justification by faith. As we said in
Chapter Two, at the root of this doctrine is the claim that
Christ reigns mysteriously and invisibly over the kingdom
of conscience, and no human authority may dare to
interpose itself as the mediator of this rule; it is by faith

alone that we participate in this kingdom, so we must not be deceived into identifying it with external works or rituals. So long as we Protestants insist on the necessity of this truth, we must continue to proclaim, and to apply anew in each generation, the Reformation doctrine of Christ's two kingdoms.

BIBLIOGRAPHY

Avis, Paul D.L. "Moses and the Magistrate: A Study in the Rise of Protestant Legalism." *Ecclesiastical History* 149 (1975): 148–72.

Bahnsen, Greg. *Theonomy in Christian Ethics.* Phillipsburg: P&R Publishing, 1984.

Ballor, Jordan, and W. Bradford Littlejohn. "European Calvinism: Church Discipline." In *European History Online (EGO)*, edited by Irene Dingel and Johannes Paulmann. Mainz: Institute of European History [IEG], 2013. http://www.ieg-ego.eu/en/threads/ crossroads/religious-and-denominational- spaces/jordan-ballor-w-bradford-littlejohn-european- calvinism-church-discipline.

Biel, Pamela. *Doorkeepers at the House of Righteousness: Heinrich Bullinger and the Zurich Clergy, 1535-1575.* Bern: Peter Lang, 1991.

Bolliger, Daniel. "Bullinger on Church Authority: The Transformation of the Prophetic Role in Christian Ministry." In *Architect of the Reformation: An Introduction to Heinrich Bullinger, 1504-1575*, edited by Bruce Gordon and Emidio Campi, 159–77. Grand Rapids: Baker Academic, 2004.

Brachlow, Stephen. *The Communion of Saints: Radical Puritan and Separatist Ecclesiology, 1570–1625.* Oxford: Oxford University Press, 1988.

Bruenig, Elizabeth Stoker. "Christo-Capitalism or Capitalanity? David Brat's Political Theology." *Political Theology Today.* June 19, 2014. http://www.politicaltheology.com/blog/christo-capitalism/.

Calvin, John. *Commentary on the Epistles of Paul the Apostle to the Corinthians,* translated by John Pringle. 2 vols. Edinburgh: Calvin Translation Society, 1848–49.

_____. *Institutes of the Christian Religion,* edited by John T. McNeill, and translated by Ford Lewis Battles. 2 vols. Louisville: Westminster John Knox Press, 1960.

Cartwright, Thomas. *The Second Replie of Thomas Cartwright: Agaynst Master Doctor Whitgifts Second Answer Touching the Church Discipline.* [Heidelberg: 1575.]

Cavanaugh, William T. "The City: Beyond Secular Parodies." In *Radical Orthodoxy,* edited by John Milbank, Catherine Pickstock, and Graham Ward, 182–200. Abingdon: Routledge, 1999.

Cranz, F. Edward. *An Essay on the Development of Luther's Thought on Law, Justice, and Society.* Cambridge, MA: Harvard University Press, 1959.

Davis, Kenneth R. "No Discipline, No Church: An Anabaptist Contribution to the Reformed Tradition." *The Sixteenth Century Journal* 13, no. 4 (1982): 43–58.

Estes, James M. *Peace, Order, and the Glory of God: Secular Authority and the Church in the Thought of Luther and Melanchthon, 1518–1559.* Leiden: Brill, 2005.

Fulford, Andrew. *Jesus and Pacifism: An Exegetical and Historical Investigation.* Moscow, ID: The Davenant Press, 2016.

Gazal, Andre A. *Scripture and Royal Supremacy in Tudor England: The Use of Old Testament Historical Narrative.* Lewiston: Edwin Mellen Press, 2013.

Gutierrez, Gustavo. *A Theology of Liberation: History, Politics, and Salvation,* translated by John Eagleson. Maryknoll, NY: Orbis, 1973.

Hart, Darryl. *From Billy Graham to Sarah Palin: Evangelicals and the Betrayal of American Conservatism.* Grand Rapids: Eerdmans, 2011.

_____. *A Secular Faith: Why Christianity Favors the Separation of Church and State.* Chicago: Ivan R. Dee, 2006.

_____. "With Friends Like These." Oldlife.org. July 20, 2015. https://oldlife.org/2015/07/20/with-friends-like-these/

Hooker, Richard. *The Lawes of Ecclesiasticall Politie.* Edited by John Keble in *The Works of that Learned and Judicious Divine Mr. Richard Hooker: with an Account of His Life and Death by Isaac Walton* [1836]. Revised by R.W. Church and Francis Paget. Oxford: Oxford University Press, 1888. Available at the Online Library of Liberty: http://oll.libertyfund.org/titles/hooker-the-works-of-richard-hooker-vol-1, http://oll.libertyfund.org/titles/hooker-the-works-of-richard-hooker-vol-2, and http://oll.libertyfund.org/titles/hooker-the-works-of-richard-hooker-vol-3.

Horton, Michael. *Christless Christianity: The Alternative Gospel of the American Church.* Grand Rapids: Baker, 2008.

Kelly, Douglas F. *The Emergence of Liberty in the Modern World: The Influence of Calvin on Five Governments From the 16th Through 18th Centuries.* Phillipsburg, NJ: P&R Publishing, 1992.

Jones, Douglas M. *Dismissing Jesus: How we Evade the Way of the Cross*. Eugene, OR: Cascade, 2013.

Jordan, James B. *The Sociology of the Church: Essays in Reconstruction*, reprint. Eugene, OR: Wipf and Stock, 1999. First published 1986 by Geneva Ministries.

Kingdon, Robert M. "Social Control and Political Control in Calvin's Geneva." In *Die Reformation in Deutschland und Europa: Interpretationen und Debatten*, edited by Hans. R. Guggisberg and Gottfried G. Krodel. Gütersloh: Gütersloher Verlagshaus, 1993.

Kirby, W.J. Torrance. *Richard Hooker's Doctrine of the Royal Supremacy*. Leiden: Brill, 1990.

———. "Peter Martyr Vermigli and Pope Boniface VIII: The Difference Between Civil and Ecclesiastical Power." In *Peter Martyr Vermigli and the European Reformations*, edited by Frank A. James III, 291–304. Leiden: Brill, 2004.

———. "Political Theology: The Godly Prince." In *A Companion to Peter Martyr Vermigli*, edited by W.J. Torrance Kirby, Frank A. James III, and Emidio Campi, 401–22. Leiden: Brill, 2009.

Leeman, Jonathan. *Political Church: The Local Assembly as Embassy of Christ's Rule*. Downer's Grove, IL: IVP Academic, 2016.

Leithart, Peter J. *The End of Protestantism: Pursuing Unity in a Fragmented Church*. Grand Rapids: Brazos, 2016.

Lewis, Gillian. "Calvinism in Geneva in the Time of Calvin and of Beza (1541–1605)." In *International Calvinism, 1541–1715*, edited by Menna Prestwich, 39–70. Oxford: Oxford University Press, 1985.

Littlejohn, W. Bradford. "Dependent or Independent? Towards a Christian Way of Thinking about Saving and Wealth." *Journal of Markets and Morality* 19, no. 2 (Winter 2016): 389–99.

_____. *The Peril and Promise of Christian Liberty: Richard Hooker, the Puritans, and Protestant Political Theology.* Grand Rapids: Eerdmans, 2017.

_____. *Richard Hooker: A Companion to His Life and Work.* Eugene, OR: Cascade, 2015.

_____. "The Search for a Reformed Hooker." *Reformation & Renaissance Review* 16, no. 1 (2014): 68–82.

Littlejohn, W. Bradford, Brian Marr, and Bradley Belschner, eds. *A Christian Theory of Law: A Modernization of Book I of Richard Hooker's Laws of Ecclesiastical Polity.* Moscow, ID: The Davenant Press, 2017.

Littlejohn, W. Bradford, and Scott N. Kindred-Barnes, eds. *Richard Hooker and Reformed Orthodoxy.* Göttingen: Vandenhoeck and Ruprecht, 2017.

Luther, Martin. *The Freedom of a Christian*, translated by W.A. Lambert, and revised by Harold J. Grimm. In *Luther: Three Treatises.* 2nd revised edition. Minneapolis: Fortress Press, 1970.

Marsilius of Padua. *The Defender of the Peace*, edited by Annabel Brett. Cambridge Texts in the History of Political Thought. Cambridge: Cambridge University Press, 2005.

Maruyama, Tadataka. *The Ecclesiology of Theodore Beza: The Reform of the True Church.* Geneva: Librairie Droz, 1978.

McIlhenny, Ryan C., ed. *Kingdoms Apart: Engaging the Two Kingdoms Perspective.* Phillipsburg, NJ: P&R Publishing, 2012.

Nelson, Eric. *The Hebrew Republic: Jewish Sources and the Transformation of European Political Thought.* Cambridge, MA: Harvard University Press, 2010.

O'Donovan, Oliver and Joan Lockwood O'Donovan, eds. *From Irenaeus to Grotius: A Sourcebook in Christian Political Thought, 100–1625.* Grand Rapids: Eerdmans, 1999.

Olson, Jeannine E. *Calvin and Social Welfare: Deacons and the Bourse Francaise.* Selinsgrove, PA: Susquehanna University Press, 1988.

Plantinga, Cornelius. *Engaging God's World: A Christian Vision of Faith, Learning, and Living.* Grand Rapids: Eerdmans, 2002.

Richards, Jay. *Money, Greed, and God: Why Capitalism is the Solution, Not the Problem.* New York: HarperCollins, 2009.

Ritenour, Shawn. *Foundations of Economics: A Christian View.* Eugene, OR: Wipf and Stock Publishers, 2010.

Rushdoony, Rousas John. *The Institutes of Biblical Law.* Phillipsburg, NJ: P&R Publishing, 1973.

Sattler, Michael. *The Brotherly Agreement of a Number of Children of God Concerning Seven Articles.* Translated by J.C. Wenger. http://www.anabaptists.org/history/the-schleitheim-confession.html.

Tanner, Kathryn. *Economy of Grace.* Minneapolis: Fortress, 2005.

Thompson, W.D.J. Cargill. "The 'Two Kingdoms' and the 'Two Regiments': Some Problems of Luther's Zwei-Reiche-Lehre." *The Journal of Theological Studies* 20, no. 1 (1969): 164–85.

Tuininga, Matthew J. *Calvin's Political Theology and the Public Engagement of the Church: Christ's Two Kingdoms*. Cambridge: Cambridge University Press, 2017.

VanDrunen, David. "Calvin, Kuyper, and 'Christian Culture'." In *Always Reformed: Essays in Honor of W. Robert Godfrey*, ed. R. Scott Clark and Joel E. Kim. Escondido, CA: Westminster Seminary California, 2010.

_____. *Divine Covenants and Moral Order: A Biblical Theology of Natural Law*. Grand Rapids: Eerdmans, 2015.

_____. *Living in God's Two Kingdoms: A Biblical Vision for Christianity and Culture*. Wheaton, IL: Crossway, 2010.

_____. *Natural Law and the Two Kingdoms: A Study in the Development of Reformed Social Thought*. Emory University Studies in Law and Religion. Grand Rapids: Eerdmans, 2010.

Wedgeworth, Steven. "Two Kingdoms Critique." *Credenda/Agenda*. June 21, 2010. http://www.credenda.org/index.php/Theology/two-kingdoms-critique.html.

Wedgeworth, Steven, and Peter Escalante. "John Calvin and the Two Kingdoms—Part 1." *The Calvinist International*. May 29, 2012. https://calvinistinternational.com/2012/05/29/calvin-2k-1/.

_____. "John Calvin and the Two Kingdoms—Part 2." *The Calvinist International*. May 29, 2012. https://calvinistinternational.com/2012/05/29/calvin-2k-2/.

Winship, Michael P. *Godly Republicanism: Puritans, Pilgrims, and a City on a Hill*. Cambridge, MA: Harvard University Press, 2012.

Witte, John, Jr. *Law and Protestantism: The Legal Teachings of the Lutheran Reformation.* Cambridge: Cambridge University Press, 2002.

Wolters, Albert M. *Creation Regained: Biblical Basics for a Reformational Worldview.* 2nd ed. Grand Rapids: Eerdmans, 2005.

Wright, William F. *Martin Luther's Understanding of God's Two Kingdoms: A Response to the Challenge of Skepticism.* Grand Rapids: Baker Academic, 2010.